What to Do When
Good Enough
Isn't
Good Enough

The Real Deal on Perfectionism

a guide for kids

Thomas S. Greenspon, Ph.D.

free spirit
PUBLiSHiNG®

Helping kids
help themselves™
since 1983

Library of Congress Cataloging-in-Publication Data

Greenspon, Thomas S., 1942–

What to do when good enough isn't good enough : the real deal on perfectionism / Thomas S. Greenspon.

    p. cm.—(What to do when)

    Includes index.

    ISBN-13: 978-1-57542-234-3

    ISBN-10: 1-57542-234-4

1. Perfectionism (Personality trait)—Juvenile literature. I. Title.

    BF698.35.P47G75 2007

    155.4'18232—dc22

2006034077

At the time of this book's publication, all facts and figures cited are the most current available. All telephone numbers, addresses, and Web site URLs are accurate and active; all publications, organizations, Web sites, and other resources exist as described in this book; and all have been verified as of January 2007. The author and Free Spirit Publishing make no warranty or guarantee concerning the information and materials given out by organizations or content found at Web sites, and we are not responsible for any changes that occur after this book's publication. If you find an error or believe that a resource listed here is not as described, please contact Free Spirit Publishing. Parents, teachers, and other adults: We strongly urge you to monitor children's use of the Internet.

The concepts, ideas, procedures, and suggestions contained in this book are not intended as a substitute for professional help or therapy.

"A backpack filled with bricks" reprinted by permission of International Creative Management, Inc. Copyright © 2005 by Anna Quindlen.

"Trying to Do Well vs. Perfectionism" chart on pages 36–37 is adapted from *Perfectionism: What's Bad About Being Too Good?* by Miriam Adderholdt, Ph.D., and Jan Goldberg (Free Spirit Publishing, 1999). Used with permission of the publisher.

Edited by Eric Braun
Illustrated by Michael Chesworth
Cover and interior design by Marieka Heinlen

10 9 8 7 6 5 4 3 2 1
Printed in the United States of America

Free Spirit Publishing Inc.
217 Fifth Avenue North, Suite 200
Minneapolis, MN 55401-1299
(612) 338-2068
help4kids@freespirit.com
www.freespirit.com

Free Spirit Publishing is a member of the Green Press Initiative, and we're committed to printing our books on recycled paper containing a minimum of 30% post consumer waste (PCW). For every ton of books printed on 30% PCW recycled paper, we save 5.1 trees, 2,100 gallons of water, 114 gallons of oil, 18 pounds of air pollution, 1,230 kilowatt hours of energy, and .9 cubic yards of landfill space. At Free Spirit it's our goal to nurture not only young people, but nature too!

Printed on recycled paper
including 30%
post-consumer waste

green
press
INITIATIVE

Contents

Dedication

This book is dedicated to Lily Adele Holker, and to Baby Two.

Acknowledgments

Heartfelt thanks to the many parents and young people who have offered their questions and insights on perfectionism over the years. Special thanks to my editor, Eric Braun, for his probing questions and his respect for my message, for which I accept full responsibility, and to my wife and professional partner, Barbara Chain Greenspon, for a decades-long intense and fruitful peer consultation.

Introduction

Has this ever happened to you? The teacher hands back your book report and you got an A minus, which is a great grade—right? But somebody else in class got an A, and that little minus haunts you the rest of the week. You act grumpy to your family and you can't stop worrying that the teacher thinks you're stupid. You might even call your*self* stupid.

Or how about this: you have to turn in a social studies project in one week, but every time you start it something seems wrong so you rip it up and start over. As the due date gets closer, you worry more and more, but you still can't seem to get started. Every time you try, it isn't good enough. The worrying gets so bad you can't sleep well. Finally, the night before you have to turn it in, you stay up late throwing something together that could have been way better if you'd just started earlier.

Are you afraid to try new things because you might not be good at them? Are you afraid to speak up in groups because you might say something stupid? Do you get really upset when people criticize you?

All of these things can be signs of **perfectionism,** and many people experience them. Perfectionism can make a person feel lots of pressure, worry, fear, and even anger. And it can be exhausting.

1

People who know about their perfectionism will sometimes say it is a burden to them. It's like an annoying noise in the background all the time, or a heavy weight on their shoulders. A famous writer, Anna Quindlen, has talked about her own perfectionism as a "backpack full of bricks." What makes perfectionism such a burden is the almost constant fear and worry about how well you're doing. You're *always* on the alert, because there might be something you forgot . . . or one more thing you should do . . . or something you just did that is not quite right. No wonder perfectionism can be exhausting! Every perfectionist has a fear, deep inside, of not being good enough—of not being acceptable to others—and it's always there. That's a heavy load to carry around, and one that can prevent you from relaxing, being happy, and doing your best.

The good news is that you *can* lighten your load. With time and a willingness to change, you can learn to have less worry and fear and feel good enough no matter how well you do at things. *And you can do just as well as you always have.* Lightening the load of perfectionism doesn't mean thinking it's okay to do a crummy job at anything. It just means worrying less about how you do.

I want to help you make the burden of perfectionism lighter. I am a psychologist, and I have helped
many kids and their families with their perfectionism. Over the years I have learned a lot about what
perfectionism is and where it comes from. The things
that helped those kids and families are the things
that are in this book—they can help you too!

Sneak Preview (What's Inside This Book)

Part 1 of *What to Do When Good Enough Isn't Good
Enough* focuses on what perfectionism is, how it
affects your life, and what you can do to make life
easier and more fun for yourself.

- Chapter 1 shows you how perfectionists **act,
  think,** and **feel,** so you can see just what
  "perfectionism" means. Some pencil-and-
  paper exercises help you decide how much
  of a problem perfectionism is for you.

- Chapter 2 explains how trying to do things well
  is different from being a perfectionist.

- Chapter 3 has seven "Load Lighteners," or
  coping skills you can use to feel better any time.

- Chapter 4 explains how people become
  perfectionists. It also explains something
  called your "self-view" and what role that
  plays in perfectionism.

■ Chapter 5 has some pencil-and-paper activities to help you learn to think of yourself differently, so you can accept yourself without having to be perfect.

■ Chapter 6 is a really important chapter that shows you how to get your parents or other trusted adults to help. Overcoming perfectionism is easier if you can talk about it with people who are important to you.

■ Chapter 7 discusses some of the ways to keep handling your perfectionism in the future. It's hard work overcoming perfectionism, and you will have ups and downs. This chapter suggests ways to keep at it, even through the downs.

Part 2 focuses on bigger issues that can be hard to handle on your own.

■ Chapter 8 discusses other problems that can sometimes get mixed up with perfectionism, or make it worse. Perfectionists often worry a lot or feel sad and hopeless, and sometimes this means there are other things going on besides perfectionism. You'll learn how to tell if this is true for you, and what to do if it is.

■ Chapter 9 explains what it's like to go to counseling. If you have one of the problems described in chapter 8, or if you're having a very hard time with perfectionism, you'll learn how an expert can help.

Lightening the load of perfectionism is a process, not just one thing that you do, and it takes time. You can begin the process by reading this book so you can understand perfectionism, how it affects you, and how you can start changing things for the better. Next, you can do the activities in this book, which include talking to the important adults in your life about how you see yourself and how they see you. What's great about these activities is that you can't pass or fail them, and you can't do *well* or *poorly* on them. If you pay attention to the suggestions, and try them, things will begin to change for the better—and that's what's *really* great. Every time you do one of these activities, you are removing another brick from that perfectionism backpack.

Keep a journal to do the written activities. You can use a notebook, do them on a computer, or write on sheets of loose paper. If you use loose paper, put the sheets in a folder so you can keep them together.

Some of the activities are for you to do by yourself, and some are for you to do with others. You might work with friends, teachers, or relatives outside your home, but it's probably most helpful to talk with your parents*. Ask your parents or another adult helper to join you as you work on easing your perfectionism. Ask them to read this book with you, especially the "Note to Grown-ups" at the end (you can read that, too). You will be thinking about yourself a lot, and I hope the adults who support you will think about themselves as well. Talking about these things together will help everyone.

The most important part of this process is that you keep on doing these activities and having these conversations. Over time, you'll lighten the load of perfectionism, brick by brick. You'll learn that you have lots to offer and that it is possible for people to accept you for who you are, rather than just for what you can do. You don't have to be perfect to be acceptable.

Even though this process takes time and involves talking to others, there are things you can do on your own right now to feel better. If

*A Note About "Parents": Many kids have two parents living at home and many kids don't, so when I talk about "parents," I mean the trusted adults who have the most to do with your life and who you feel closest to. When you see the word "parents"—or "mom or dad"—think of the person or people in your life who fit that description. This might mean biological parents, stepparents, adoptive parents, a single parent, grandparents, other adult relatives, or friends you live with. To make things simple, I'll just say "parents," because "adult caregivers" sounds like I think you live in a zoo!

perfectionism has you feeling worried or pressured right now, see "Chapter 3: Load Lighteners."

If you are reading these words, you're already starting the process of easing the burden of your perfectionism. The fact that you are interested in learning about this, and that you might be willing to do something about it, means you can succeed. All you have to do now is stick with it. Many kids and adults have overcome their never-good-enough feelings using the ideas in this book, and *you* can, too.

I'd like to know how this book helps you. I'd also like to know if something here is puzzling to you or if you would like to know more. You can email me at help4kids@freespirit.com or send me a letter at:

Free Spirit Publishing
217 Fifth Avenue North, Suite 200
Minneapolis, MN 55401-1299

Be sure to send me your address, so I can write back to you. Best of luck on your journey!

Dr. Tom Greenspon

Part 1

Getting to Know Your Never-Good-Enough Feelings

Chapter 1

What It's Like When Good Enough Isn't Good Enough

As it gets close to bedtime, ten-year-old **Jason** is putting everything he needs for school the next day in a particular order on his bedroom floor: books, pencil case, pack of tissues, and so on. That way he can load up his backpack and his pockets in the right order in the morning, and he'll be absolutely sure he hasn't forgotten something. Jason worries a lot about whether he will remember everything. He likes to do things in a certain way every time. It feels comfortable to him, and it means he can always be sure that whatever he is doing will turn out just right. But tonight, while Jason runs downstairs to get a notebook he needs, his brother comes into the bedroom and moves some things aside so he can play a card game in that spot. He moves everything neatly, but to Jason that doesn't matter. When he comes back he is furious at his brother for touching his stuff and screams at him.

■ ■ ■

Eleven-year-old **Kristin** is feeling stuck as she stares at the computer screen. She has a history report to write and it seems like she has started

9

it a hundred times. She has a stack of note cards on her desk. She has read everything she can think of to read about the Stamp Act of 1765, but she worries that she still doesn't know all she could. She writes a paragraph and reads it. It doesn't seem quite right, but she can't figure out exactly why, so she deletes it and thinks some more about how it should start. She writes a couple sentences, but these don't look right either. She worries that her report will never be good enough.

Do either of these stories sound familiar? Do you worry a lot about getting things right? Does it seem like things you do are not quite good enough a lot of the time?

For some kids, like Jason and Kristin, it feels like nothing can be right unless it's perfect. It feels like getting things to be perfect is the only way to be satisfied. But very few things in life actually *can* be perfect, so these kids are unsatisfied—and unhappy—most of the time.

Perfectionism and Fear

Perfectionism is wanting to be perfect, especially at things you do. If you feel that "good enough" isn't good enough, that nothing less than totally perfect will do, then you're probably a **perfectionist.**

There's more to it than that, though. Perfectionism is not just wanting to do things perfectly. Perfectionists also feel fear about NOT being perfect. Most people like to do things well—even perfectly. But as you know, people are human, and that means they can't always do things well! Most of the time, "perfect" is impossible. People make mistakes, and they fall short of perfect, because they're human.

For many people, being imperfect is not a big deal. They can say, "Oh well, I'll try to do better next time." But perfectionists have trouble with that "oh well" part. Perfectionists think making a mistake means there's something wrong with them. They're afraid people won't like them or accept them if something is wrong with them. So being less-than-perfect is scary to think about. Everyone wants to be liked and accepted.

For a perfectionist, the fear of not being accepted is almost always there. That's what creates the burden you read about in the "Introduction." It can feel like carrying around a backpack full of bricks all the time.

How Perfectionism Affects You

In this chapter you'll learn what perfectionism is like. Then you'll start to learn how much of a problem perfectionism is for you and how exactly it affects your life. As you do this, you're already starting the process of changing things for the better.

The next few pages tell about the ways many perfectionists **act, think,** and **feel.** Some of the things may be true for you, too. As you read about them, you can start your own lists of actions, thoughts, and feelings—lists that describe what perfectionism is like for *you*.

How Perfectionists Act

Here are some of the ways perfectionists act. Do you do any of these things?

Agree to do way too many things at the same time

Always have to win

Rarely let others help with a project

Say things like, "How could I be so stupid?" or "That was really dumb" when they do something imperfectly

Arrive late to school, parties, or events because one more thing had to be done

Have a hard time making choices

Frequently criticize others

Always compare their work to the work of others

Wait to do things until the last minute (this is called **procrastination**)

Always have to be in control

Get carried away with the details

Always do last-minute cramming to get things done

Pay more attention to negative than positive comments

Never seem satisfied with their work

Keep constantly busy

What does this list tell you about perfectionists? Lots of things. Here are three of the big ones:

They're Overloaded

If you have to do everything, and you have to do it all yourself, then you have an awful lot to do—especially if you have to do it all perfectly. Even when perfectionists let someone help them, they have to go back and check the person's work to make sure it's

perfect. And it always seems like there is at least one more thing to do before something feels finished.

They Worry

In addition to the weight of everything perfectionists think they have to do, perfectionists worry that none of it will get done the way it should. Even if they do a great job on something, they can't enjoy it. They might have 20 people compliment them on their work, but they'll be awake in the middle of the night worrying about the *one* person who said, "It's okay, I guess"—and ignoring the 20 compliments!

Many perfectionists worry a lot about details. When that happens, the load gets heavier still because there can be *lots* of details, including ones that probably don't matter. The report is done and you finally like what it says—or at least you're okay with it—but which

Not every overloaded perfectionist *looks* overloaded. For some, it's important to do everything, to do it all perfectly, and to look like they have everything totally under control with no worries or stress. The perfect image!

font should you use to print it out? Should the page number be at the top or at the bottom? Two spaces between the title and your name, or three? Or five?

Shari, who is ten, sits down to make a poster that will go with her science project for school. She gets out all of her colored markers and puts them in place, and then she thinks for a while. She gets an idea, takes three of the markers and carefully draws a picture of a sun to go with some paragraphs about the solar system she has printed out. The picture isn't quite right, though. It needs a little more red, and should be slightly more to the left. So she throws it on the floor and starts over, on another sheet of poster board. But it's a little too big this time, and she throws it away again and starts over. This happens several times. To her mom, it looks like Shari is driving herself crazy.

Have you ever done what Shari is doing? You start something—like a project for school—and after a while you decide it just isn't right, so you throw it away and start over. And then the same thing happens again. And then it happens again. You can't stop worrying that there is something wrong each time you try.

They Run Out of Time

Perfectionists often run out of time to do things, sometimes rushing at the last minute. That's because making sure everything is perfect is not only exhausting and stressful, it takes a lot of time as well.

Gerald is eleven. He is a whiz at math, but he has big problems taking tests that have a time limit—as most tests do. When he gets a test, Gerald starts at the beginning and digs into the first problem. He thinks about it and does the work he needs to do. Then he wonders, "Is this right?" Even though he's great at math, he just can't be sure. So he erases some of his work and figures it out again. Then he thinks about it and changes it again. When he finally is satisfied with the answer, he moves on to the second problem. He carefully calculates the answer, but then he does the same thing he did with the first problem: he second-guesses himself. He erases part of his work and does it over a couple times. Finally it's on to the third problem. Same thing. Soon time is up. Most of the kids in class have completed the test, but Gerald has done only half of the problems.

Another reason perfectionists run out of time is because they **procrastinate.** Procrastination is when you put things off until later . . . and later, and later.

Charlie, age thirteen, is always feeling pressured by deadlines. He gets an assignment in school or volunteers for a project in his church youth group, and at first he's very excited about these things . . . but then days go by when he doesn't do anything about them. He can't seem to get started. As the deadlines near, he starts to worry. The dates get closer and closer, and he gets more and more upset and overwhelmed. He just can't make himself settle down to do the assignment, and he keeps thinking about how he won't have enough time to do it in a way that will satisfy him—perfectly. Of course, that makes it harder to get started. Eventually, he ends up turning in sloppy work that he did at the last minute, and he feels terrible.

It may seem like a perfectionist wouldn't put things off, since getting everything done right is so important. So why do some perfectionists procrastinate? Because perfectionists are afraid of having their work judged. If there's a chance that maybe, just maybe, someone might judge their work as not quite perfect, it can be hard to start that work. As long as they don't do it, the possibility of perfection is out there. It almost seems better to skip their school project and get a zero on it than hand it in and risk getting a B. Or even an A minus.

You don't deserve that kind of punishment. If you notice that you're putting pressure on yourself the way Charlie, Gerald, or Shari do, try to give yourself a break. For example:

- Check your work just once, and move on.

- Break down big projects into parts and plan when you'll do each part. That way you'll feel less overwhelmed.

  To learn more ways to give yourself a break, check out Chapter 3: Load Lighteners, on pages 40–47.

- Reward yourself when you turn in something on time—get a milkshake with friends or watch a movie.

- The next time people offer to help, let them!

How Do You Act? Make a List of Your Own

Take out your journal and write this title at the top of the page: "Perfectionistic Ways I Act."

Under the title, start a list of perfectionistic things you do by looking at pages 12–13 and copying any of the items that apply to you. Then add any new items you can think of. Maybe something on that list got your attention, but it wasn't exactly true for you. How would you change it so that it describes you better? Or, maybe something you've read in this book has made you think of something else that isn't here. Put that on the list, too.

Write down as many things as you can think of, then put the list away for a while. You'll probably think of more to add later, so try not to worry about making it perfect! For now, it's just important to start thinking about this. It might not seem like making a list can help you, but it can. Just by learning to see the way perfectionism affects you, you are starting the process of lightening the load. It makes you more aware and helps you know and understand yourself a little better.

Important! With this list, you are starting your journal process. Keep your notebook or notes handy, because you'll use the list again and write more lists, too: lists that describe what you think and feel. Remember, what you write in the journal isn't a school assignment or a test, so you can't fail it. Whatever you put down is okay. Do your best to relax and think honestly about yourself.

How Perfectionists Think

Everyone carries on conversations with themselves inside their head. This is called "self-talk." (Some people might even do a part of their self-talk out loud.) Perfectionists typically have a certain kind of self-talk. What might perfectionists be saying to themselves? Here are some examples:

I should excel at everything I do.

I should finish a job before doing anything else.

I can't do anything right.

People shouldn't criticize me; it means I did something wrong.

I always have to stay ahead of others.

I'm a wonderful person if I do well; I'm a lousy person if I do poorly.

Things should be done right the first time.

Every detail of a job should be perfect.

If I goof up, something's wrong with me.

I'm stupid.

I'd better not make a mistake or people will think I'm not very (smart, good, capable).

If I can't do it perfectly, what's the point?

Everything should be clearly black or white, right or wrong.

No one could really like me.

There is only one right way to do things.

Looking at those words, you can feel how hard perfectionists are on themselves. There are a lot of "shoulds"—like, I should do everything perfectly, I should do it right the first time, I should be better than everyone else. It's like a set of rules perfectionists have for themselves. There are also lots of worries: I'm never good enough, I'm stupid, I'd better not make a mistake, no one likes me.

Between the "shoulds" and the worries, perfectionists end up pushing themselves very hard, and they end up judging themselves pretty hard, too.

Possibly the most important item on this list is the one that says "I'm never good enough." To a perfectionist's way of thinking, he or she is never good enough, and there is never a time to just relax and say, "Okay, I'm done with this job and I like it." A perfectionist never gets to be satisfied with a job well done. That's a really important part of life. To a perfectionist, "good enough" sounds like leaving something unfinished. It can't be good enough—it has to be *perfect*. The thing is, perfection is difficult or impossible, so perfectionists feel lousy about coming up short most of the time.

Can you ever be good enough? Let's say you are a runner. You finish a race in your best time ever. You win, but you didn't break the state record for your age level. Is that good enough?

What if you lose, but both you and the winner *do* break the state record? Good enough?

Okay, what if you win, and you break the state record, but not the national record?

When does it get good enough?

The problem isn't that you aren't good enough. The problem is with the whole idea of "good enough."

If you lose a race, could you ever be proud of yourself 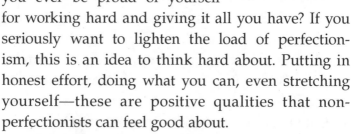 for working hard and giving it all you have? If you seriously want to lighten the load of perfectionism, this is an idea to think hard about. Putting in honest effort, doing what you can, even stretching yourself—these are positive qualities that non-perfectionists can feel good about.

"Good enough" isn't a way of saying anything will do. It means you have actually arrived at a goal. You have done your best and that's good. If you think this way about it, you can be good enough and still lose. You didn't win the race, or you didn't make an A, or you flubbed a note in your guitar recital. You worked hard, though, and you plan to keep at it, and you'd like to improve. Thinking this way, you probably *will* improve. You can be completely proud of that.

Losing hurts. No one is saying it should be just fine to lose or mess up or make mistakes. Of course you want to make things better. The point is, mistakes don't say anything about *you as a person*, except that you are human.

Believing you are good enough is not a way of accepting second best. It's a way of being comfortable with who you are.

Thanh is really excited to work on a model stock car he got for a present. It sits on a table in his bedroom, waiting to be built. But instead of working on the model, he starts a cleanup project in his room, getting everything straight and tidy. His room is already pretty clean—it usually is—especially for a twelve-year-old. No one has asked him to clean up now, but he likes to have things in order. Thanh thinks, "I really want to build this model, but the first step is to get my room straight. There's only one right way to do this, and that means taking care of my room first." But Thanh can't say exactly *why* straightening up the room needs to be first.

■ ■ ■

April is in sixth grade, but it's hard for her to be in class, or to be in a group of people who are talking about something, because she believes she isn't very smart. That's why she never speaks up in class or with friends: she's afraid she might say something that proves she's dumb. She actually does well in school, but she says to herself, "That's just because the work is really easy" or "I just got lucky." Why does she think she isn't very smart? Because sometimes she makes mistakes. "If you're really smart," she thinks, "you don't make mistakes. Mistakes are what stupid people do!" April thinks smart people are able to figure things out right away, and they always know enough to get the right answer the first time.

Thanh and April are both very hard on themselves. Thanh believes things need to be done in a certain way or else they won't turn out well. He believes that if he does things the right way then everything will be okay. So he lives by a strict set of rules, telling himself he *has* to do things *just so*.

But Thanh could treat himself a lot better by changing his self-talk. For example, what if Thanh's self-talk went more like this: "Finally, I've got the time to build this stock car. I'm going to dive right in; my room is a little messy but I'll get to that later. I'm really good about keeping it clean anyway, so that's not a problem, and I've been looking forward to working on this car all week." Thanh would be a lot more relaxed if he could speak this way to himself.

For April, the problem isn't doing things in a certain way, it's what she thinks about herself. She tells herself she isn't smart, and she says she knows this because smart people don't make mistakes. She compares herself to others and she always sees them as brighter than she is, even though she actually does well in school. What if she said to herself, like some people do: "I do fine in school, so I'm okay in the brains department. Some people do better than me, but that's the way it is—some people do worse." If April could find a way to say this to herself, life would be easier for her. She might even speak up more in school and with friends.

If you're hard on yourself in the ways described here, you can change your self-talk, too. You deserve to be treated kindly, especially by you! The next time you notice yourself thinking something like, "I'm stupid" or "I'm no good at math," try changing that thought to something kinder, like, "Math is hard for me, but I'm good at other subjects" or "I didn't do as well as I'd like on this test, so next time I'll study harder."

How Do You Think? Make a List of Your Own

Open a new page in your journal and write this at the top of the page: "Perfectionistic Thoughts I Have."

Under the title, start a list of your own perfectionistic thoughts. Some of your perfectionistic thoughts might be the same as the thoughts on page 20.

Others might be totally different. Think about your list, write down as many ideas as you can, and then keep the list handy in case you think of something new later.

How Perfectionists Feel

Besides certain actions and thoughts, perfectionists have certain feelings as well. Feeling exhausted and overloaded are common ones. Here are some others:

Deeply embarrassed about mistakes big or small

Afraid of being rejected or left out

Anxious and nervous when giving an opinion

Often worried about details

Angry if a routine is interrupted and they can't do things the way they like to

Ashamed of having fears

Afraid of appearing stupid

Exhausted and unable to relax

Constantly upset with themselves for not being able to do things just right

Disgusted or angry with themselves whenever others criticize them

Often fearful or anxious

Earlier, you read about how perfectionism and fear go together. You can see lots of fear on this list: fear that you won't be good enough, fear that you'll sound stupid, fear that things won't go the way they're supposed to, fear that people won't like you or respect you very much. It's no wonder perfectionism is such a burden—all those fears weigh a lot!

The fears of perfectionism actually can *prevent* you from doing your best. That's because fears paralyze you—they stop you in your tracks. Fears keep you from trying things or being creative. If you're too busy making sure nothing bad happens to you, it's hard to make something good happen.

Shawn is at his friend's house with a group of boys. They are talking about the recycling discussion they've been having in their seventh-grade class. André is arguing that recycling isn't worth the trouble because not enough people do it. But Al disagrees. He says, "We have to work to save the planet." Shawn agrees with Al: he thinks a person should do his part, whether others do or not. In this conversation, though, Shawn isn't saying anything. He knows André or someone else might disagree with him. He's afraid he'll look stupid, or people will laugh at him.

■ ■ ■

Johanna's fourth-grade class is getting their spelling tests back from the teacher. When Johanna gets hers, she sees that she spelled 19 out of 20 words correctly. Her friend Adrian leans across the aisle, holding out her test, and says, "We both got 19 right—cool!" Adrian is beaming about the score and feeling really good about how she did. She looks up the missed word, repeats it a couple of times, and settles down to listen to what the teacher is saying.

Johanna is in a different world. She's not even thinking about getting 19 words right. Instead, she feels awful about the one she missed. She feels depressed about not getting a perfect score and angry with herself for not being good enough. She is embarrassed to have turned in such poor work to the teacher, and she's afraid the teacher and everyone else is going to think she's stupid. All of these feelings make it difficult to pay attention, and she hardly hears what the teacher is saying now. This happens a lot to Johanna. Mistakes always seem like more than just mistakes, and she feels really bad about them.

Perfectionists can spend a lot of time feeling bad. They often feel stupid or like something's wrong with them in some way, and they're embarrassed because of that. They may be angry when things don't go right, and they may feel hopeless that things will ever change. And there is the fear. *What will happen if I do this or don't do that?* Johanna is so afraid of mistakes that she can't even think about how well she did on her test. It's like the words she spelled right don't exist.

How Do You Feel? Make a List of Your Own

Turn to a new page in your journal and write this title at the top of the page: "Perfectionistic Feelings I Have." Then start your own list of perfectionistic feelings. You can use the list of feelings on page 26 to help you get started.

Next to each feeling on your list, add a note of how often you feel this way. Most of the time? Once a day? Once a week? Also, see if you can remember how long the feelings last. Do you get over bad feelings in a couple of minutes, or does it take a couple of hours? Or a couple of days? Longer? You want to see how much of your time you spend feeling bad about yourself.

Remember, as you learn about the way perfectionism affects you, you are learning to understand
yourself better, and you are lightening the load of
perfectionism.

Brick by Brick

The three lists you made of ways you act, think, and
feel are lists of your perfectionism traits. Read them
again and think about how they affect your life. Does
perfectionism make things harder for you a lot of
the time? Do you often feel bad because of negative
self-talk? Are there many times when worry and fear
keep you from doing new things or having fun?

There's no certain number of traits that makes
you a perfectionist or not a perfectionist. It's more
likely you are a perfectionist if you have lots of traits,
but you might want to address your perfectionism
even if you have only one or two traits on each list.
You didn't make these lists to measure your perfectionism like some kind of test score, you made them
to help you learn more about yourself. If the traits
on your lists bother you, or make life harder for you,
then you can do something about them.

By reading this book and making these lists,
you have already started doing something. You
have begun the process of lightening the load of

perfectionism. As you continue to read, you'll learn more about perfectionism and where it comes from. You'll learn how to practice thinking in new ways and expecting new things from yourself. You will learn to work on these things for yourself, but you also will learn how to get your parents or other important adults to help you. This process can take a long time, but it's worth the reward of feeling relaxed, confident, and acceptable for who you are.

■ ■ ■

Looking this closely at your perfectionism might feel scary or sad. As you go through this process, your journal can help. You don't have to use it only for the activities in this book. A journal is a private place to keep track of your ideas, feelings, and thoughts. You can use it to write what's going on in your life or how you feel about the things you're learning in this book. You can draw pictures if you prefer. Doing this can help you dis-cover more about how you feel, and it can help you work through problems.

Chapter 2

What's the Difference Between Perfectionism and Trying to Do Well?

Tamara, thirteen, has always loved ballet. She has been taking lessons since she was four, and recently she's started to think about making it her career. Tamara is a good student and she has friends, but she spends a lot of her time practicing ballet and watching videos of dancers. When a recital is coming up, you'll find her in the living room practicing. Tonight, dinner is ready but Tamara's not at the table, so her dad has to go remind her. When he walks into the living room, Tamara doesn't even notice him. Her expression is very serious, but calm. She misses a step, stops and repeats it until she is satisfied, and then moves on. Her dad practically has to stand in front of her to get her attention, but when he does, she smiles, turns off the music, grabs a towel, and says, "Okay, let's go!"

Is Tamara a perfectionist?

Well, she is working very hard and she is focusing on one thing in her life. It's even more intense when a recital is coming up. She clearly wants her performance to be just right.

So, is she or isn't she a perfectionist?

To figure out this puzzle, you need to know the difference between perfectionism and trying to do well. To help you see the difference between these two, take a look at the following list.

These Things Are NOT Perfectionism:

- working very hard on something, and even overworking for a little while to get something done

- pushing yourself to do your very best on something, and having high standards for what is acceptable

- looking at your mistakes, and working to avoid them in the future

Anyone who really wants to do well at something will spend a lot of time and energy getting it just right. That's not perfectionism. That's wanting to do the best you can. Perfectionism is wanting something to be *perfect*—not just the best you can do. And remember, perfectionism also is being afraid or worried that something *won't* be perfect.

You may have heard people say something like, "I'm a real perfectionist," but what they usually mean is they work very hard to get things right. That's not perfectionism. A *real* real perfectionist is someone who wants things to be *perfect*, and who is always afraid their best won't be good enough.

As you continue reading Tamara's story, see if you can tell whether she's a perfectionist.

Tamara is in the middle of her ballet recital. She is relaxed but concentrating on what she is doing, when suddenly she comes out of a *pirouette*—a turn—on the wrong beat. Without hesitating, she goes on with the rest of the routine. Afterward, she is disappointed and feels bad about the mistake. But she also remembers that the rest of her performance went very well. Her teacher gives her a hug and says she's really proud of how Tamara handled herself, especially the way she continued to do so well after the mistake.

Tamara is focused on doing well, not on being perfect. She works hard to do well. But she also can accept her mistakes, and she sees that she is getting better. She feels disappointed—and sometimes even frustrated and angry—when she doesn't do as well as she had hoped. But she does not beat up on herself when that happens.

So, Tamara is very good at what she does, she works hard at it, and when she makes a mistake she learns what she can from it and keeps on going. Tamara is not a perfectionist.

In chapter 1 you learned that fear is a big part of perfectionism. That is true even when things are going well. Most people are proud when they do things well, but perfectionists aren't. They're *still afraid*. They're worried that things haven't gone well enough. Being proud of your accomplishments is healthy and important and feels really good. Perfectionists rarely get to feel that.

Trying to Do Well

Trying to Do Well

Doing the research you have to do for a project, working hard on it, turning it in on time, and feeling good about what you learned.

Studying for a test, taking it with confidence, and feeling good about your score of 9 out of 10, or getting a B+ instead of an A.

Choosing to work on group projects because you enjoy learning from different people's experiences and ways of doing things.

Accepting an award with pride, even though your name is misspelled on it. (You know it can be fixed later.)

Getting together with people who are interesting, likable, and fun to be with.

Being willing to try new things, even when they're a little scary, and learning from your experiences and mistakes.

Keeping your room cleaner and neater, making your bed more often, and putting your clothes away.

Joining a soccer team and playing two or three times a week to have fun and compete with other teams.

vs. Perfectionism

Perfectionism

Writing your report over three times, staying up two nights in a row, and handing it in late because you had to get it right (and still feeling bad about your report).

Cramming at the last minute, taking the test with sweaty palms, and feeling bad about your B+ because a friend got an A.

Always working alone because no one can do as good a job as you—and you're not about to let anyone else slide by on *your* A.

Being grumpy about the award because the officials didn't get your name right.

Refusing to be with people who aren't star athletes, smart, and popular.

Avoiding experiences because you are terrified of making mistakes—especially in public.

Not being able to leave the room until the bed and room are just so.

Taking lessons as often as you can, practicing every day, and not feeling satisfied until you can beat every other team in your league.

Can you feel the differences between the two lists on pages 36–37? When you try your best, you go after *excellence*, not perfection. Trying your best is working hard and feeling good about how things are going. Perfectionism is overworking, worrying about all the details, and feeling terrible when something doesn't go perfectly. Trying your best also means trying new things, even if they seem a little scary, so you have a chance to learn or accomplish things you never did before. Perfectionists are afraid to try new things.

Is Perfectionism Ever Helpful?

Nope. No way. Never.

Some people may feel proud of their perfectionism and believe it makes them successful. But if you understand it for what it really is, you can see that it simply gets in your way. Perfectionism is a worry and a burden. It's never helpful.

Some people think, "I'm afraid that if I lose my perfectionism, I won't be good at things any more." But if those people can step back and think about their talents and the hard work they do, they will realize that they aren't good at things because of their perfectionism. If they could wave a magic wand and remove their perfectionism, they would still be good at things. That's because their success comes from their talent, their energy, and their commitment.

The same is true for you. If you are successful at something, it's because of the skills and talents you have developed, plus the effort you put in, plus your determination to do well. All your perfectionism does is add a lot of worry. If you are a perfectionist, you aren't a success *because of* your perfectionism. You're a success *in spite of* your perfectionism.

Here's something else perfectionism isn't: it isn't an emotional disorder or a mental illness. Sometimes perfectionists also can experience depression or anxiety, which are emotional disorders. But perfectionism is separate and should be dealt with separately. Go to chapter 8 to learn more about these other problems.

skills + talents + effort + determination = success

■ ■ ■

Trying to do your best isn't a bad thing, even if you're a perfectionist. The more you practice thinking about your perfectionism as something that gets in the way of doing your best, the more success you'll have.

Chapter 3

Load Lighteners

Imagine your town or community is putting on a carnival or a fair with lots of fun games, like a three-legged race, a scavenger hunt, and a water balloon toss. There are even a lot of tasty snacks, like popcorn and funnel cakes. Everyone is having a great time . . . but you have a backpack full of bricks on your back. The games are a lot harder for you, and they're not really fun. Even eating snacks and talking to friends is hard, because the weight of those bricks makes you uncomfortable.

As you read in chapter 1, being a perfectionist is like wearing a backpack full of bricks all the time. Some people have had it on so long, they don't even realize how much it's pulling them down. Even if they are aware of it, they might think that's just how life is, and there's nothing they can do. But there *are* things you can do to lighten the load and enjoy yourself more.

This chapter describes seven of those things. I call them **"Load Lighteners"**—strategies you can use to take a brick or two out of your backpack right now. They'll help you feel less burdened by worry so you can enjoy the fun things in life.

Using Load Lighteners

You can use these Load Lighteners at home, at school, when playing or practicing, or any time you feel fear or worry about how well you're doing. They'll help you cope with your feelings so you can feel better about yourself. The Load Lighteners are numbered, but you don't have to do them in any order. Try as many of them as you like and see which ones work best. The more you do, and the more often you do them, the better you will feel.

#1: Dive In

Are you the kind of perfectionist who often procrastinates? Somewhere deep inside, do you secretly fear getting started on things because you don't want to face the thought of doing a less-than-perfect job? If so, start something—like your math homework, an art project, or your blog entry—right now, before you feel totally prepared. You can always go back later and make changes. After you dive in once, try it again with something else you've been putting off. The more times you dive in, the easier it will become for you to start things. And maybe—just maybe—knowing you weren't as prepared as you could have been will free you up to do a less-than-perfect job, but still a job you can be proud of.

#2: Not "Right," Just Write

Use the journal you started in chapter 1 to do other activities in this book, especially the ones in chapter 5. But your journal isn't just a place to do activities. It can also be a private place to write about your thoughts and feelings as you work on lightening the load of your perfectionism. Or just to write about what's going on in your life, or to draw pictures.

When you write about your thoughts and feelings, you can learn to understand them better. You might learn things about yourself you didn't know, and you can even figure out solutions to problems you have. Over time, as you do the activities in this book and work on your perfectionism, your thoughts and feelings will change. If you record your thoughts and feelings in your journal, you can see that things *are* getting better, even if sometimes it doesn't *seem* like things are getting better.

Here are some things you can write about:

- Make a list of things that help you relax and worry less.

- Write about something you did well.

- If you're worried about a big project coming up, write about that. Break the project into smaller parts and make a plan for doing each part.

- When are you happiest? Write about it.

Remember, there's no right or wrong way to write in your journal—you just do it!

#3: Crack Up

Next time you feel stressed about doing well on something, or about what others might think of you, find something to laugh at. The more laughing you do, the better. Laughter releases chemicals called "endorphins" in your body that make you feel better. It's also good exercise—you use most of your muscles to laugh! All of this can help take your stress level down and give you more energy to face your work. Relaxation and humor can help you try things even if you are scared or worried about what might happen.

Here are a few ways to get you cracking up. You can probably think of others, too:

- Watch your favorite funny movie.

- Read a funny book or Web site.

- Draw a silly picture.

- Call a friend who's funny.

- With friends or siblings, make up a goofy play and perform it—just for yourselves.

#4: Move It

The fear and worry that go along with perfectionism can put a lot of stress on your body. Some kids get headaches or stomachaches, and some feel burned out, tense, crabby, or tired. If you feel lousy in any of these ways, or if you just want to have something to take your mind off the fear and worry, get active. Exercise is a healthy way to burn off some of that stress. It helps you release nervous energy and clear your mind.

You probably have some favorite ways you like to exercise. Here are some ideas you might add to your list:

- Run around the block.

- Play basketball at the park.

- Walk your dog (if you don't have a dog, ask if you can walk a neighbor's dog).

- Ride a skateboard, bike, or inline skates.

- Go swimming with friends or family.

- Do active chores: sweep the kitchen, dust, rake leaves, or shovel snow.

- Do jumping jacks in your living room.

- Dance to your favorite music.

#5: Imagine Someone Else Did It

If you're mad at yourself for doing something less-than-perfectly, imagine someone else did it instead. For example, let's say you get a disappointing grade on a test, give up the losing goal as a hockey goalie, or lose a fantasy football game, and you feel really bad about it. You might even think you're some kind of loser for letting this happen.

Take a minute to pretend it wasn't you. It was a friend or someone in your class who made the mistake. What would you think of that person?

Now, imagine something else. Imagine that person, besides getting a disappointing grade like you, also does all the good things you do, too. He or she tries hard, cares about improving, and sometimes gets higher grades. Imagine that person, like you, also is friendly and caring. What would you think of that person now? Would you think he or she is not good enough? Probably not. Probably, you'd be a lot easier on that person than you are on yourself. You deserve the same treatment!

Do this exercise every time you start getting down on yourself for not being good enough. It will get easier and easier to see yourself in a way that is more fair to you.

#6: Just Say No

You read in chapter 1 how many perfectionists are overloaded. They try to do too many things, and they try to do them all perfectly. Here's something you can do to lighten your load: the next time someone asks you to volunteer to do something, try saying, "Sorry, but I'm really busy right now and I can't do it. Thanks for asking, though!" Make sure you are polite but firm. Setting limits for yourself is a way of taking care of yourself.

Important note: Some things that are part of everyday living you usually can't say no to, like homework and chores around the house! You can still say no to other things, though.

#7: Do Something That Can't Be Judged

Sometimes it feels like everything you do is either good or bad. If you need a break from worrying about how well you're doing at things, do something that *can't* be done well—OR poorly. Watch a favorite TV show, for example. You can't do that badly. Here are some other ideas:

- Take a walk.

- Email a friend just to say hello.

- Read a book.

- Call a grandparent.

- Play with a younger sibling, or color or do a puzzle (don't compete!).

- Go to a playground.

- Listen to music.

- Write in your journal.

All these are positive things to do because they help you feel good—and some of them make others feel good, too. And no matter how things turn out, you can't do them poorly. Enjoy the positive feelings!

■ ■ ■

Tell your friends and family about the Load Lighteners, and ask for help when you need it. Show them how you've done some of the activities— maybe they'd like to do some of them with you!

Chapter 4

Where Does Perfectionism Come From?

Why do perfectionists act, think, and feel the way they do? As with all kids and adults, it depends on what they believe about themselves and the world around them.

Daryl, age eleven, is always excited about helping his dad with a project in the woodshed. His dad takes the time to show Daryl how to adjust the machines for cutting or shaping pieces of wood, and they talk about measuring and marking the wood to get it to be the right size. Daryl has learned a lot about math this way, although it hasn't been called "math." It's just how you figure out the way wood needs to be cut. Daryl feels like a helper to his dad, who says, "Thanks for giving me a hand with this shelf repair. This is fun. We're a real team." Daryl feels great about himself. He knows he can do lots of things when it comes to woodwork, and he likes to try other things, too, and believes he can learn to do them well. With this positive view, Daryl tends to think good thoughts

48

about himself: he is competent, capable, and helpful. He has good feelings as well: he is proud of himself and happy about what he can do. He gets along well with his dad and this helps him in his relationships with other people, too.

■ ■ ■

Twelve-year-old **Lisa** likes to play softball. She plays catcher on a traveling team, and the coach says she has talent. Her dad was a catcher, too, and he helps his daughter practice hitting and fielding every weekend and attends all her games. During one game, Lisa gets three hits and plays a really good game behind home plate. She even throws out a baserunner trying to steal second base. After the game, her dad seems irritated and says, "That was a good game, but you let a low pitch get past you again. You have to do better at blocking those, or you'll never make it in high school ball." Lisa feels bad and wonders if she really has it in her to be a good catcher. Is she really any good at softball? Does her dad think she can ever learn? *Can* she ever learn? Lisa figures that if she can't catch, she can't do a lot of other things, either. Her thoughts about herself are not very positive. She has a negative **self-view.**

Your Self-View

Your self-view is the way you see yourself and your relationships with others. It has a lot to do with how you act, think, and feel. A positive self-view means you like yourself as you are. If you have a positive self-view, it is easier for you to try new things. That's because you believe a mistake isn't terrible—it's just a mistake. Most of the time you can learn from it and go on. People liked you before you made the mistake, and they will like you afterward, too. The more positive your self-view, the more likely you are to be relaxed, feel good, and make healthy choices.

A negative self-view means you *don't* like yourself as you are. You think of yourself as not good enough. If you have a negative self-view, you find it harder to try new things. That's because if you make a mistake—or get a poor result—you believe it would prove there's something wrong with you. You think people might not like you anymore.

Where Does Your Self-View Come From?

When people are very young, they do a lot of things because they are interesting, or because they want to copy someone else who has done them. That's how we learn to do things like talk and walk, and later on to joke and sing, or run and jump. Sometimes we do these things well, and sometimes we don't. As we do them, we are learning about the world around us.

At the same time, there are usually other people with us who watch what we're doing, or who play with us while we are doing it. These people are usually our parents or other family adults, childcare providers, or family friends. What they say to us at this time, and the way they act, tells us something about ourselves. They might say things like "Good job!" or "No, no!" They might smile or frown or take a toy away or give us a hug—and so on. From these reactions, we learn what the adults think of as the right and wrong ways to do things.

But that's not all we're learning. Over time, we're also learning what these adults think of us, and that affects what we think of *ourselves*. We're forming our self-view.

If the adults with us say mostly encouraging things, like, "Let me show you how to do this," and then they let us try it again, we start to understand that they think we can do it. We also learn that they like us and are interested in helping us. We start to have confidence in ourselves and in our relationships with others.

But what if, as we go about our business of playing, the adults with us make a lot of negative comments, like, "No, that's not the way to do it!" or "Stop that!"? What if they seem irritated with us for not doing something right? What if they tell us not to do it, or they just don't help? For one thing, we wouldn't be learning how to do things well. But also, after a while, we might start to believe we aren't very good at things. We might even start to think something is wrong with us, or that the important adults in our life have given up on us and don't think we are worth helping. Our self-view will begin to get very negative.

Your self-view begins to form as soon as you are born, and it continues to develop as you grow older. The adults who are most important in your

People are human and most of them criticize sometimes. But if you feel overwhelmed by harsh criticism, or if you feel like you're in danger of being physically hurt by adults in your home, talk to an adult you trust. This could be a family grown-up outside your home such as a grandparent, or a teacher, principal, counselor, coach, or family friend. That person can help you figure out what to do. If you need help right away, call 911.

life can have a lot to do with this. At times when they seem pleased with you, or glad to have you around, you will probably feel good about yourself. You will believe people can like you for who you are. At other times, if important adults are upset or angry with you, you may feel silly or bad. You may even believe you are not likable. Everyone has a mixture of these positive and negative times as they grow up. If people experience more of one than the other, their overall view of themselves can get to be almost totally positive, or almost totally negative.

The adults in your immediate family aren't the only adults who can influence your self-view. Many times aunts and uncles, grandparents, teachers, religious leaders, coaches, bandleaders, scoutmasters, or other adults besides your parents can have a big influence in your life as well. These are all people who may be close to you in some way. If you look to them for help and guidance, and if you trust them and admire them, then they are important to you, and you like to feel important to them.

Think back to the two stories at the beginning of this chapter. Daryl has a good feeling about himself. He feels capable and likable. He will probably continue to learn new things and to believe he is able to do some things very well. What about Lisa? She is beginning to wonder about herself, and about whether she is really acceptable as a person. She might become discouraged and just give up. She might quit playing softball, and she also might quit doing much of anything. She might become very discouraged about her life, and she might even become depressed.

A person who becomes depressed feels sad, hopeless, and helpless a lot of the time. If you feel this way now, talk with an adult about it as soon as you can. You can talk to a parent, another family member, a teacher, someone in your religious community, or any other adult you trust. Let the adult know how you are feeling so he or she can help.

There is another thing that Lisa might do, though, instead of giving up. She might work hard to please her father. If he's very hard to please, Lisa might start to believe she has to be perfect to satisfy him. Then she would be on her way to perfectionism.

How Perfectionism Begins

Most parents love their kids. They want what is best for their kids, and they try to protect them from getting hurt. Sometimes, though, even the most loving parents can send messages they don't mean to send. For example, parents who work hard to protect their kids from making mistakes and getting hurt may accidentally teach their kids that mistakes are unacceptable.

If kids get the message that they need to be perfect in order to be acceptable, then that's probably what they'll try to do. There are lots of ways kids might get that message. Here are some examples.

Kids might think they need to be perfect if the important adults in their lives:

- **Criticize them a lot.** If kids often feel negatively judged by family adults, they may try harder and harder to satisfy them. It begins to seem like the only way to satisfy them is to be perfect.

- **Criticize others a lot.** In some families, adults have lots of complaints about others, like people they work with or politicians. The children don't want to be like these people their parents don't seem to like, so they try hard to be perfect to stay safe from criticism.

- **Do lots of things *for* them.** In some families, it seems like the grown-ups want everything done faster and better, and they don't let kids do many things for themselves. These kids might start to think they *can't* do things very well, and they might work hard to be perfect so they can feel like they *can*.

- **Compare one child in the family to another.** If grown-ups often say things like, "Why can't you be more like your brother?" kids may start to feel not-good-enough. Then they might try to be perfect in order to feel confident and smart.

- **Don't say much at all about kids' behavior.** Sometimes when this happens it can seem like no one really cares about the kids one way or the other. Then kids might think they aren't really important. They might try to be perfect, just so they will be noticed and feel important.

- **Have very strict rules about how to behave.** In these homes, it might be hard to relax and play. Kids might not get lots of hugs or kind words. Then they might start to wonder whether the

You may have heard that being gifted and talented also can cause perfectionism. But so far, research has found that gifted and talented kids are not more likely to be perfectionists than other kids are. Gifted kids often have high standards and want to do exceptionally well, but that's different from perfectionism.

Gifted kids who are perfectionists often have a chance to display their perfectionism in a public way because of their ability to do well—maybe even perfectly—in school. Because this is so public, it *may seem* like more gifted kids are perfectionists.

grown-ups are glad the kids are there. Kids might try to be perfect so they won't get in trouble.

- **Are perfectionists.** Kids might learn to be perfectionists by copying their parents' behavior.

- **Say, "Yes, but" a lot.** Or maybe, "That's good, but," or "That's okay, but." For example, "Yes, it's good you did your homework tonight, but you should *want* to do it." Or, "The B on this test is okay, but why didn't you get an A?" Kids in a family like this might think "good enough" means nothing less than perfect.

- **Have a home that doesn't feel safe or calm.** In some families there is lots of fighting and arguing. Maybe someone drinks too much alcohol, or maybe there is violence. Sometimes kids in homes like this try to be perfect because they believe it can make all of the bad things better.

If you feel like you're in danger of being physically hurt by adults in your home, talk to an adult you trust. This could be a family grown-up, a teacher, principal, counselor, coach, or family friend. That person can help you figure out what to do. If you need help right away, call 911.

It's Not About Blame

Most parents don't intend to make their children into perfectionists. Like you, your parents do things because of the way they understand the world, and the way they see themselves. Parents also have a self-view, just like you and everyone else. They grew up in homes where this self-view started. Your parents' own parents, and other important adults in their lives, helped form it. Your parents' self-view has a lot to do with how they act as parents. All parents bring their own ideas to the job of parenting, doing whatever they feel is the best thing to do.

In chapter 6, you'll have a chance to ask your parents about their self-views and how they might have become the people they became.

It's important to be very clear about this:

No one, including you, is "to blame" for your perfectionism.

You can't overcome perfectionism by blaming someone for it. This chapter is not about blame, it's about trying to understand your perfectionism so you can make things better. When you understand where your self-view (and your perfectionism) comes from, you can begin to understand this important fact:

Your self-view is not who you ARE—it's just a way you learned to look at yourself.

And even though you can't simply decide to change your self-view—like flipping a switch—there is a way to make it different. Many perfectionists have done it. They have learned to lighten their load, and you can, too.

Chapter 5

Going Further: Thinking Differently About Yourself

If you are a perfectionist, you probably have two ways of thinking about yourself:

- Sometimes you think: "I'm good at what I do— maybe better than most people."

- Sometimes you think: "I'm never good enough, and I'm always one slip away from failure."

If you put them both together, you end up with, "I may be good, but I'm never good enough."

If you could somehow change these ideas about yourself, you could get past your perfectionism. The problem is, changing your self-view can be like changing your ideas about how the world works—sort of like getting yourself to believe you can breathe under water. It's a known fact of the universe that people can't breathe under water, and it may seem like a known fact of the universe that you are never good enough.

No one in history has ever breathed under water, and without SCUBA gear, no one ever will. But there are plenty of people who know they aren't perfect and still believe they are good enough. They may be interested in improving themselves, but they believe they are good  enough as they are. You can become one of these people. You can begin by working to understand your self-view, questioning why it is the way it is, and then working to change it.

One Way of Looking at Yourself

As you read in chapter 4, your self-view is made up of all the ideas and feelings you have about who you are and how you fit in with others. Your self-view *seems* to be the true and real and final facts about yourself: it's just the way things are. Right?

Actually it's *not* final. Your self-view is just one possible way of looking at yourself. If you had a different self-view, you would look at yourself differently—but you'd still be the same person.

Think about these questions:

- If you take a break from practicing the cello (or violin, or basketball, or something else), are you relaxing or being lazy?

- If you get a B or an A-, is that a good grade or not so good because it's not an A? Is it a failure of some kind?

- If you do make A's in school, is it because you're smart, or because you work hard, or because you get lucky, or because the work is easy . . . or some combination of these? If you are lucky, does that mean you aren't also smart?

If you believe taking a break from practicing is being lazy—even though you have just been practicing very hard—then some people would say you're being too hard on yourself. Some perfectionists would like to rest from the constant work of trying to be perfect, but then they think of themselves as lazy for wanting to rest.

What about your grades? You have to be smart to get an A in school—if you think you got an A only because you got lucky, that means you don't see yourself as very smart. And that means you are pretty hard on yourself. You have a negative self-view.

Dan and Keisha's Story

Dan and Keisha are friends. They've lived next door to each other since kindergarten, and they're thirteen now, so they've known each other a long time. Because of that, Dan feels comfortable talking to Keisha about a lot of things. Lately they have been reading the same series of books and talking about them. One afternoon, sitting in front of their building, Keisha says, "I think the books are about having friends."

"Even more than that," Dan says, "I think they're about being loyal to those friends."

Keisha agrees. They keep talking, and they laugh together about the funny parts. They both know all of the characters and all of the details about the places described in the books.

The next day at recess, Dan and Keisha find several kids who are talking about the same books. Everyone is telling about their favorite parts, and Keisha joins right in. She is comfortable talking in groups like this, because she feels smart and capable. Everyone listens to her and agrees with what she says.

Dan is excited about the conversation, but he doesn't say anything. He's afraid to speak up because he doesn't feel smart or capable. He never speaks up in groups because he's afraid he might look foolish, or someone might disagree with him—and that would seem to prove that he isn't smart. When Keisha says, "Dan, tell them your idea about being loyal to friends," Dan says, "Nah—you tell it. You know better than me."

After school that day, as Keisha and Dan are walking home, they have this conversation.

Keisha: Dan, are you okay?

Dan: Sure, why?

Keisha: Well, when the other kids were talking about the books, you seemed like you were in some other world. You didn't say anything, and I know you love to talk with me about them.

Dan: Well, I didn't have much to add.

Keisha: What do you mean? You talked for an hour about the same stuff yesterday! You have tons to add!

Dan and Keisha have very different self-views. Even though they know the same things about the same books, Keisha is comfortable talking in a group about them and Dan is not.

Dan firmly believes that it's *true* he is not smart or capable, and every time he makes a mistake it reinforces that belief. But his friend Keisha believes he *is* smart and capable—so who's right?

In truth, neither one is right *or* wrong. These are just two points of view, or opinions, about Dan. As you learned in chapter 4, your self-view is not who you ARE—it's just a way you have learned to look at yourself.

Half-Empty and Half-Full Glasses

"Is the glass half-empty or half-full?"

Maybe you've heard that question before. Your answer can say a lot about your self-view. Do you usually focus on what you *have* or on what you *don't* have? If you are a perfectionist, you probably see the glass as half-empty. You probably focus on the negative side of things—the empty part.

Let's say you run your best time in a race, but someone beats you. If you have a negative self-view, you're more likely to say, "I lost," rather than, "I just did better than I ever did before!" Obviously, both things are true. Your point of view determines which truth you focus on. If you have a more positive self-view, you're more likely to focus on what you have done well. Of course you'll know when you've lost a race, but you'll probably see that as something that just happens in sports—not some kind of proof that you're a loser. You're more likely to think about how well you've done, even if you could still improve.

Think about how you feel when you make a mistake. Is a mistake just something that happens along the way to learning something new, or is it a sign that something is wrong with you? If you have a negative self-view, you probably think something is wrong with you when you make a mistake. That might lead you to push yourself to be perfect. But if you have a positive self-view, you feel acceptable as you are. You don't feel you have to prove yourself over and over, so it's easier to believe that mistakes are just a part of living. Okay, sometimes an annoying part, but still just a part of living!

Looking at Your Self-View

In the rest of this chapter, you'll find pencil-and-paper activities to help you look at your self-view and start to change it, so you can start to feel more acceptable as you are. If you don't have one already, it's time to get an adult helper: someone you trust who can look over the activities with you and show you what to do. These activities may bring up some feelings that are hard to handle alone. Dealing with these feelings will be easier if you have an adult to guide and support you. If it isn't possible for a family grown-up to help, ask your teacher or your school counselor.

You already started a journal in chapter 1. If you also have been doing any of the journaling ideas on pages 42–43, that's great. You can use the same journal for all the activities in this chapter.

What's Good About You?

Make a list of your positive qualities. You can title it, "What's Good About Me." To help you get started, take a look at the following list and see if any of these qualities fit for you.

Many perfectionists are people who:

- have a sense of responsibility

- take things seriously

- are very organized

- are proud of what they accomplish

- are willing to put in effort in whatever they do

- have a sense of independence

- have high standards

- try to correct mistakes and do things well

- make sure jobs are finished

- are willing to look at themselves and make changes

- are considerate of what
  others think about them

- take criticism seriously

- want to be prepared for whatever job needs
  to be done

Put any of these items on your list if they fit for you. Then add as many new ideas as you can think of. Putting your positive qualities on paper is a great way to see them clearly and start thinking of yourself as good enough. Keep your list where you can look at it often—like taped to the wall next to your bed, or taped inside your school binder. Remember to look at it. This is who you are. You will probably think of more things later, and if you do, add them.

As you look at your list, ask yourself: If you met somebody with all of these positive qualities, what would you think of that person? Would he or she seem like an interesting person? Would you like to know that person? Even with all of those good qualities, would you think that person still isn't good enough? Would you demand that he or she be perfect?

What Would Happen?

What would happen if you did something that was less than perfect?

Turn to a new page in your journal and write "What Would Happen?" at the top. Then write all the things you can think of that might happen if you made a mistake or did something that wasn't perfect. What if you made a mistake in a soccer game or did poorly on a spelling test? Would the world end? Would you collapse in a heap? Would you be embarrassed to death?

Okay, those are jokes. But on a more serious note: Would someone complain? Would someone be angry with you?

If someone were to say something to you about your mistake, who would say it? What would that person say?

Be honest with yourself about what you think will happen if you goof up. Whatever that is, making yourself perfect is what you've been doing to avoid it. When you write it down and look at it on the page, it can begin to seem less scary.

The Putting-Aside-What-You're-Doing Experiment

Are you the kind of perfectionist who feels you have to finish what you start before moving on to something else, no matter how important the other thing might be? If so, try this: The next time you're doing

something and there's a good reason to do something else, set aside
what you are doing and go to the
next thing. Let's say you are doing
a puzzle—or working on the
computer—and it's time to
eat. Put everything in a safe
place, or save your work, and
eat. When you've finished eating, go back to what
you were doing.

After you've done that, take out your journal and
write about how you felt when you put aside whatever you were doing. Were you uncomfortable? Was
it hard to do? Most people like to finish what they
start, and interruptions can be annoying, but if you
are a perfectionist, it feels worse than that. Sometimes
it seems like everything will be all messed up if you
don't finish what you are doing. It seems like there
will be too many loose ends and you might forget
something. It's good to finish things and not let them
go, especially if they're important, but most things
don't have to be finished immediately. They can wait
while something more important gets done.

After you finish writing about that, write how
you felt after you returned to the first thing you
were doing. Did you feel bad that you left it? Or was
everything fine?

This experiment can show you it's okay to leave
something and come back to it. It challenges you to

do things differently despite your fears. Maybe next time you have to leave one thing to get something else done, it won't seem so hard. Maybe you can do it again.

The Check-Your-Work-Once Experiment

Have you ever done this? You finish an assignment for school and you check it over to see if you missed anything or to see if it's done the way you like it. Then, do you go back over it again, just to see if it's right? And then, do you do it again? And again? If you do this sort of thing, try something that might seem scary: The next time you finish an assignment, check your work only once. Then put it away until you hand it in. As you put the assignment away, notice how it feels to let go of it. Is it hard to do? Why? What do you think will happen if you don't check your work one more time?

Get out your journal and write about how you felt checking your work only once.

It's important to check the work you do to make sure you didn't overlook something, but a repeated nervous search of every last detail doesn't help you do better work. It only adds worry to your life. If you have a lot of trouble thinking things are "done," then ask yourself what "perfect" would look like. And ask yourself why it is that small details give you such big worries. These are questions to answer in your journal.

This experiment, just like the last one, can help you see that you can make changes, and you'll be okay. Maybe it will start to seem less scary to turn in your work without checking it so many times. Maybe you can do this the next time you have to turn in an assignment. And the time after that.

The Putting-Your-Dummy-on-Display Experiment

We all have a "dummy" inside us. It's that little person we seem to become every time we do something we think is really stupid or embarrassing. If you're a perfectionist, you may feel like you are actually the dummy, and maybe if you're lucky there is a smart person inside of you who shows up every once in a while for just a minute. If you feel this way, you're

probably afraid to do new things because you're afraid to put your dummy on display.

Take this challenge: do something you ordinarily would never do because you are afraid you'll look stupid. Maybe it's playing miniature golf, or dancing with someone, or playing a new video game, or singing a song for someone, or ice skating, or doing an art project, or joining the kids who play football at recess, or reading something you wrote in front of the class, or raising your hand in class to answer a question from the teacher. Whatever—pick something you're afraid might make you look stupid, and try it. Do you remember Dan from the story earlier in this chapter? His challenge would be to say something he is thinking the next time he is in a group.

Before you do this experiment, take out your journal and write what you think will happen when you do it. Do you think everyone will look at you? Do you think someone will laugh?

Next, do the new thing—ice skating, speaking up in a group, or whatever you chose. After you've done it, go back to your page and write what happened. What did this experiment feel like for you? Was it horrible? Did it feel like everyone was watching you and laughing? Were you embarrassed? Or was it really fun? Or something in between horrible and really fun? Was there any difference between what you thought would happen and what actually happened? If so, make sure to write about that.

Here's an important question: If you don't do well at something right away, can it be fun anyway? Write down your answer.

If you had fun doing this experiment, think about doing it again. Maybe you can try another new activity, or maybe the one you did this time was so fun you'd like to do it again. Either way is great. Most of the time, when you try something new, it's not as scary as you thought it would be. If you keep trying new things, your fear will begin to ease up.

If you try this experiment and it turns out bad for some reason, even that can be helpful. You faced your fear and you made it through! You can still try it again, and your fear can still ease up a little each time.

A New Self-View

These activities can help you learn more about how you see yourself. Keep doing the activities, keep the notes you've made, and keep thinking about these things. Each time you do an activity, compare your journal notes to the last time you did it. Can you begin seeing yourself differently?

Experiments like these (maybe you can think of others to do as well) are meant to raise questions in your mind while you take the risk of doing something new. Do you have to do things only a certain way? Does everything have to be perfect? Who says?

What really happens if you do things differently, or do something new?

If you can remember your "What's Good About Me" list, and you can start believing that terrible things won't happen if you do things in a new way, then you can see yourself differently. Over time, good enough will begin to seem good enough.

■ ■ ■

Ask a parent or an adult helper to support you while you do these activities, especially when the activities seem scary or hard. Talk to the adult about what you've learned. And remember: the more you do these activities, the easier they will become—and the closer you'll be to looking at yourself in a new way.

Chapter 6

Getting Help from Family and Trusted Adults

Your ideas about who you are and where you fit in are influenced by what you believe other important people think of you. It makes sense, then, to talk to these important people and get their help.

Talking to others helps you in several ways.

- It helps you get information you need.

- It makes your relationship with the person you're talking to stronger.

- It gets you and the other person thinking about things like how you do (or don't) get along. Many positive changes can happen after that.

- It helps you feel acceptable and important to the other person.

Here's an example of how talking can help. Sometimes you might wonder what your parents think about something. Maybe you wonder how they would feel about you if you got a B instead of an A. Or, what if you failed something?

Would they be mad? Scared? Would they stop loving you? Would they think less of you?

There's one way for you to find out the answers to these questions. Instead of wondering and worrying about it—ask! Your parents probably will tell you what they are thinking, and your questions might start a conversation that can change your relationship. Your questions could also open up new ideas for your parents, since they may not have thought about these things before.

You and your parents will have new things to think about, and talking about them together makes for a new kind of relationship. All because you asked.

There's one other really good thing about talking, and it doesn't matter who you talk to or how much talking the other person does: it builds your self-confidence. It can be scary to organize your thoughts and say them out loud, because you are putting yourself out in the open. But overcoming the fear and doing it anyway feels good and helps you to feel like your thoughts are important. The more confidence you have, the less you feel you need to be perfect.

Of course, just like your parents, you have some thoughts and feelings that you would rather keep to yourself. That's fine. Everyone has private thoughts, and you can decide if you ever want to talk about these thoughts with your parents or anyone else.

Who to Talk To

Your parents or other adults in your family are probably the people most directly concerned about you, and they are the ones most likely to influence your self-view, so that's the best place to start. If you can't talk to your parents, talk to the adult you're closest to. That might be a teacher, a religious leader, an aunt or uncle, or even an adult friend who is important to you. If you've talked with an adult helper for earlier chapters in this book, that's a good person to talk to now. If your adult helper hasn't seen this book, you can ask him or her to read it and then talk with you about it.

What to Talk About

Here are six topics you can discuss with a parent or other important adult. Start with the one that seems most comfortable for you, and then try others.

Topic 1: What's Good About You

In chapter 5, you made a list of positive things about yourself. Maybe you've added to it since then. Whether your list is long or short, it can be very helpful to hear ideas from others about what else could be added. Show your parents or adult helper your list and ask what they think about it. Then ask if they can think of anything to add.

Kaitlin is nine and is reading the same book you're reading right now. She's making a list of things that she feels are likable about herself. This is what she has on the list so far:

	What's Good About Me
	• I work really hard on things like school assignments.
	• I am pretty good at soccer.
	• I pay close attention to details when doing any job.
	• It's important to me to do well.
	• I am a loyal friend.

Her dad is in the kitchen, so she asks him what he thinks about her list.

Her dad says, "Yep, I think that's a pretty fair list you have. I would agree with all of it."

Kaitlin feels good about that, so she says, "Great— thanks!" Then she adds, "I was wondering if you can think of anything else that might go on this list? Anything I didn't think of?"

"Well," says her dad, "I know you usually finish things you start. Mom and I have talked about how much we appreciate that!"

"Wow, thanks!" Kaitlin says as she sits down to add this to her list. She thinks about all of this and reminds herself to look at her list whenever she feels down.

Kaitlin probably feels good about having her dad agree with the things on her list. If her dad, who obviously knows her well, believes these things, they just might be true. She also found out that he thinks something good about her that she hadn't even thought of. That probably feels good, too!

Topic 2: Your Perfectionistic Traits

Pull out the lists you made in chapter 1 of perfectionistic ways you act, think, and feel. Show them to your parents or adult helper and talk to them about the things you wrote down. You could start by saying:

- Could you take a look at these lists I made? What do you think about the stuff I have on here?

- Do you agree with what I wrote?

- Have you noticed other things about me that would fit on these lists?

- Do you act, think, or feel any of these ways, too?

This is a good way to get a conversation going about perfectionism in general, and about how your parents see you in particular.

Topic 3: What If You Fail

Remember the "What Would Happen?" activity you did on page 69, about what you think would happen if you didn't do well on something, or if you failed? Take that out again and show it to your adult helper or your parents and ask them what they think about your answers. You can ask:

- What do *you* think will happen if I don't do well?

- What do you think of me when I don't do well?

- Is what you think of me when I *don't* do well different from what you think when I *do* do well?

Topic 4: Is Your Parent a Perfectionist?

Do you think one of your parents might be a perfectionist? Or both parents? Ask them what they think. Talk about the lists from chapter 1 of ways a perfectionist acts, thinks, and feels, and ask if anything on the lists applies to them. Do you share some of the same qualities?

You can talk about this with an adult helper who isn't a parent, too. Sharing ideas and thoughts with others about their perfectionism is a good way to start looking at things differently.

Topic 5: Looking at Self-Views

Just like you, your adult helper or parents have a self-view. Ask them how they see themselves. Do they have some ideas about where their self-views come from? What did they think their parents expected of them? How does that compare to what they expect of you?

Topic 6: Talk About This Book

Maybe a family adult or other grown-up asked you to read this book. One way to start a conversation is to ask why he or she gave it to you—especially if that person is the parent or adult helper you've been working with. This adult probably had some particular reasons for doing it—ask what they are. If you got the book from someone else, ask your parent or adult helper to read it. Then you can talk about it together.

How to Start Talking

If you've never had conversations about important, personal topics like the ones in this chapter, then it might seem scary or hard to bring them up. It can be hard even if you *have* done it before. It might help to remember that there isn't a right or wrong way to do this. You don't have to be an expert, and you don't have to do it perfectly. Sometimes it's best to dive right in. You can say, "I've been wondering about something," or "I've been bothered about something and I wonder if we can talk about it." This will get the conversation going. After that, it doesn't matter how it got started.

The only bad way to start a conversation is to do so rudely. Saying something like, "Hey—sit down here and let me tell you something!" is probably not a good opener! It's important to show respect for the person you're talking to, which usually means *asking* to talk about your thoughts and feelings.

If someone gave you this book, that person may ask you how it's going. He or she might ask, "What do you think of the book so far?" or "What have you been learning from the book?" This is a great opportunity to talk. Say what you think. Even if you aren't very far along or aren't sure what you think yet, you could say, "I don't know yet" or "I've only read a little bit, but there is an interesting list in chapter 1." You don't have to have everything thought out and settled before you speak.

Maybe your parents or other adults have already said something to you about your perfectionism. Maybe they've noticed how hard you are on yourself at certain times. Even if you've already talked

about it a little, you can bring it up again. Say something like, "You know how you worry about me when I start something and tear it up, and then start over again? Well, I just read about that in this book. Can we talk about it?"

Here are some other ways to start:

- "I was reading this book and thinking about myself. Can we talk about it some time?"

- "You know how you're always saying I'm too hard on myself? I just read something in this book about that—can we talk about it?"

- "I have this project due in a week, and I was thinking about it. I think I'll do okay, but what if I don't? How would you feel about that? What do you think when I don't get an A?"

- "Did you want me to learn something in particular from this book on perfectionism?"

- "Okay, I'm working on this list of positive things about me, and I need your help. Could you look at my list and tell me what you think? Is there anything you might add?"

Even though there isn't a right or wrong way to have a conversation, there are some things you can do to make the conversation go better. Here are some tips:

- Find a time when you are not distracted by other things, like getting ready for school. That way you can both give the conversation all your attention.

- Don't bring up these topics when you and your parent or adult helper are arguing about something. Wait for a time when things are calm. Start by asking, "Is this an okay time to talk?" You'll both be more willing to hear each other's point of view when you start your conversation at a relaxed moment.

- Talk about what *you* are feeling or thinking, not about what you think *others* should do. For example, instead of saying, "You have to quit nagging me all the time about my grades!" you could say, "I feel really bad about myself when you remind me a lot about my grades."

- Remember to listen to others and think about what they are saying.

- If the conversation seems hard, or if people start to get angry, ask if you can talk more later on. Taking a break can help each person calm down and remember to think of the other person's feelings.

Bjorn is fidgeting at the kitchen table, worrying about a paper that is due for his seventh-grade social studies class. His mom always talks about how important it is to do well in school. His grandma and grandpa live with the family, too, and they have very high standards for school. Bjorn's older sister is a straight-A student who studies hard and always gets her work done. Bjorn works hard, too, and usually does fine, but he is always scared about his grades.

When his mom comes in the kitchen, she asks, "How's it going, Bjorn?"

Bjorn says, "Well, I'm kind of scared about handing in this paper. I'm not sure I'll get a very good grade on it, and I think you and Gram and Grandpa will be mad at me. Will you?"

His mom thinks it over and says, "We would be concerned about it because we think you are a pretty good student, but I don't think any of us would be angry. Does it seem like we would be?"

"Yeah," says Bjorn, "it seems like you are really upset if I don't get an A on something. You get all quiet, and sometimes Grandpa looks disgusted."

"Hmmm," his mom says. "I think it would be good for all of us to talk about this. I know I don't feel angry when you don't get an A, but maybe I'm doing something to make you think that. We'll see what Gram and Grandpa have to say. Thanks for bringing it up!"

Bjorn has the courage to ask a question about something that is worrying him, and it sounds like his mom, at least, is glad to talk about the problem. Lots of good things can happen now. Instead of worrying about whether his mom and grandparents get mad when he doesn't get an A on something, Bjorn can find out for sure. Maybe his mom (or grandma or grandpa) really does get mad but doesn't realize it. Maybe no one knows how worried it makes Bjorn when people get upset about his grades. If so, talking about it with Bjorn might encourage his mom and grandparents to feel differently. If they think Bjorn isn't trying hard, and Bjorn really *is* trying, then they may come to understand that. They may not be so angry next time. Change is always possible, if everyone can talk.

Bringing up subjects like this with your family can be scary. If you can get up the courage to talk, though, two important things can come out of it:

1. You can discover that there are other people who feel the same way you do—maybe even your adult helper or parents at some time in their lives.

2. You can find a solution to something that has been a problem for you. It feels great to find a solution together with others, because you feel like a team.

Family Meetings

Some families have regular meetings to talk about things. They meet once a week to talk about good things that have happened, to plan for the next week, and to talk about concerns or gripes. They also save some time to talk about what they like about each other and about being a family together. When they do this, it is easier for everyone in the family to feel safe and secure. It's easier to feel liked, and to feel listened to, and to feel accepted.

Family meetings should include the entire family. That way, everyone gets to share their thoughts, and everyone gets to hear what others are thinking. If decisions are made about things like chores or family rules or plans to do fun things, everyone has a say.

Family meetings work well when people can discuss things they are angry about, or sad about, or scared about. If everyone has the courage to say what's on their mind, and if everyone listens and is respectful of what others say, then almost any problem can be solved by working together.

If you think family meetings would be helpful in your family, talk to your family about scheduling them. Here are some guidelines to help make family meetings smooth, fun, and fair:

- Set a time when everyone is available. Many families meet at the same time every week.

- Keep the meetings short, but make sure everyone has a chance to talk.

- Include the whole family, even the baby (if you have a baby in your home).

Here are some topics you can cover:

- follow-up on topics from the last meeting that need to be discussed more

- chores, and who does them

- plans for fun

- anything important happening during the coming week

- problems anyone is having

- what people appreciate about each other, and why it's good to be part of this family (this is an important topic)

If a topic is upsetting, suggest everyone think about it some more and come back to it at the next meeting.

Your parents, and maybe other important adults, have a lot to do with the self-view you form—and they *keep having* a lot to do with it. As long as you spend time with them, they keep affecting your self-view. When you talk to them, and ask them what they are thinking, then things can begin to change for the better. Not only can you find answers to things you've wondered about and solutions to problems, but you begin to feel respected and confident. Then maybe being perfect won't seem quite as necessary.

Chapter 7

Getting Better All the Time

Sometimes, as you work on the things in this book, perfectionism might feel like something that is "wrong with you"—like a disease you should get rid of, and once you do you'll be perfect. But easing the burden of perfectionism is not about getting rid of something bad. It's about learning to judge yourself less harshly and learning to find ways to feel acceptable for who you are. Learning these things is a process that takes time, but if you keep working at it, perfectionism will grow lighter and become much less of a problem in your life.

By reading this book and doing the activities in it, you have begun that process. The next step is to keep doing these activities and keep having conversations with your parents or adult helper. Keep practicing thinking in new ways—more fairly and realistically—about yourself. Keep practicing doing things differently.

Over time, it can be easy to lose interest or to go on to other things, so in this chapter, you'll learn some ways to keep the process going through the ups *and* the downs, even when it seems confusing or hard.

Practice Makes Less-Than-Perfect

The activities in this book are not meant to be done one time only. They're meant to be practiced, so you can get better and better at doing things differently and thinking differently. If you keep practicing, you can begin to feel more acceptable. If you get discouraged—because it seems like you aren't making progress or for some other reason—here are three strategies to help you stay focused.

Expect Progress, Not Perfection!

Write this on the cover of your journal, or on a piece of paper that you can hang somewhere you can see it every day: "The journey is the goal."

Think about that: You aren't aiming to be perfectly non-perfectionistic. You are making a journey and continuing to improve—week by week, month by month, year by year. Yes, you can keep improving all of your life. And you are learning to feel acceptable while you do this. Remind yourself of that whenever you feel down about your perfectionism.

Progress rarely happens in a straight line. There are times when things go well, and times when things seem to be hard again. Imagine your progress as a spiral going up.

Sometimes it seems like you are at the same place as when you started, but you actually are a rung up on the spiral. After you have been working at this for a while, you may find yourself worrying again about some mistake you made. Notice some differences, though: maybe the worrying doesn't last quite as long, or feel quite as bad. Or maybe it's easier to talk to someone about it. That's progress.

Track Progress in Your Journal

Most people find it easier to stay focused on something when they can see that they are making progress. An easy way to see your progress is to keep all your activities from this book together in your journal. That way, when you feel like nothing is getting better, or you're just bummed out, you can go back and compare how you're feeling now to how you felt two weeks ago, or two months ago, or longer. On any particular day, it can be easy to think, "This isn't working! My perfectionism is the same as it ever was!" But if you can look in your journal and remember how you felt before, the progress you've made will be easier to see.

Remember What You Have Going for You

Remember on pages 67–68 when you made a list of positives about yourself? Look at that list every day. Keep in mind all these things you know you have going for you and what your strengths are, and keep adding to that list as you discover new good things about yourself.

Even if you try something new or hand in an assignment and it doesn't turn out well, none of the strengths you have will be changed by that. You're still the same person. Even if you make a mistake—even if you make more than one mistake—you are still the same person with all the same strengths as before. **You aren't your mistakes. You are YOU!**

Keep Talking!

Talking is healing. It's not a guarantee—sometimes talking gets difficult, and feelings are hurt. But it's still the best way to make things go better in your life.

If you've decided to talk with your parents or another adult helper about your perfectionism, here are three things you can do to make sure you *keep* talking and keep making progress.

Schedule Conversations

If you can, schedule a regular time to talk with your family or adult helper. You might do it every week at the same time and in the same place. If you have a calendar, mark the conversation date on there. Seeing it written down will make it feel more important and harder to forget about or skip.

When you have conversations, remember to say what you appreciate about each other and why you like being together (even if you don't like being together 100 percent of the time!). And keep talking about the subject of mistakes. What do people think about mistakes? Does someone get angry? Does someone get embarrassed? Does someone say you're stupid for making mistakes? Do you say this to yourself? Talk about specific mistakes you or others have made, and how each person responded to them.

Remind yourself, and each other, that all of this is a *process*. It will take time and there will be ups and downs, but it will definitely be worth it.

Talk Openly About the Hard Stuff

As you make positive changes and work to overcome perfectionism, keep in mind that amazing changes are happening. You and your family or adult helper are talking to one another differently and are thinking about things you haven't thought about before. As you learn to discuss these topics, some things will come up that you or others may be sad or even angry about. Whenever people think about how things got to be the way they are, it's understandable to have some regrets or to discover things you wish you had done differently.

Have the courage to talk about the things you've been upset about. You might say, "I was really sad when you said that" or "I really got angry back then." Or even, "When you fight a lot, it gets scary!" Since you are all talking about this together, you have already made a commitment to yourselves (and each other) to make things better. You are working as a team. Discussing the hard stuff openly can be a way of connecting with each other and finding solutions.

Celebrate What You're Doing

It's important to discuss the way things have been, and it's also important to talk about what things could be like in the future. Take time, though, to consider what is happening right now. Give yourselves high fives for what is going on in the present moment: you are talking in new ways, you are exploring each person's role in your family, you are tackling the problems of perfectionism, and you are finding ways to work together. Wow! Take some time to plan something fun and celebrate a work in progress.

Have Courage

Remember, a big part of perfectionism is fear. You're afraid that people won't like something you do, or that they'll laugh at you or not like you. Or that you'll try something and end up looking stupid. Or that you'll do something and someone else will do it better. You're afraid you will fail.

Courage is what you have when you learn to do something *even though you're scared*. You hand in an assignment even though there might have been one more thing you could have done better. You go out for hockey because it looks like fun, even though you have never played it before and you won't know how to do it right away. You say your opinion about something, even though someone else might have a different opinion.

Learning how to dive into a pool can be scary. No matter what you do to learn about it and prepare yourself for it, there will be a moment when you have to let yourself tip over and fall off the diving board. That's your moment of courage. If you are ever going to get better at something, or overcome a challenge, you will have to have your moment of courage.

It takes courage just to walk onto the diving board. That's what you have done. You've shown courage by reading this book and beginning to think differently about yourself. The next step—actually doing something differently—isn't as big as you might think.

When you're looking for your moment of courage, your "What's Good About Me?" list can help. Remember to look at that list when you need to boost your self-confidence. Another thing that helps is to remember the people who believe in you, and who believe you can do it. If you have had conversations with your family or adult helper about having to be perfect, you know you have important people in your life who will like you even if you make a mistake. Keep them in mind when you are about to try something new.

And don't forget this: perfectionism doesn't make you successful . . . YOU do. If you wave a magic wand—*whoosh!*—and get rid of all of your perfectionism, you will still be just as successful and just as likable. It's your talent, your hard work, and your energy that make you successful. Your perfectionism can only stand in the way of that by making you worry too much.

Okay, there are no magic wands. Your perfectionism will just have to dissolve slowly, as you get the courage to try new things, and as you talk with others about what they think about you. The backpack full of bricks will get lighter, brick by brick by brick.

If you do your part, that's just what will happen.

Part 2

Getting Help for Hard-to-Handle Problems

Chapter 8

Other Problems That Can Go Along with Perfectionism

For most perfectionists, a sense of order is important. Getting things just right, and making sure they stay that way, reduces the chances that anything will go wrong and mistakes will be made.

Many times, perfectionists feel hopeless about the possibility of being perfect. It seems like they will never be good enough, and that can make them very sad.

A sense of order and a feeling of sadness are normal, and for some people—including some perfectionists—those feelings can be very strong. In some cases, those strong feelings may be a sign of **emotional disorders** such as anxiety disorder or depression. An emotional disorder is what professionals call it when someone's emotions (or feelings), thoughts, or behaviors seem unpredictable and hard to control, and when they get in the way of normal living a lot of the time. Trying to deal with your perfectionism is hard enough, but how do you know if you might also be experiencing an emotional disorder in addition?

And if you are, what should you do? In this chapter you'll learn about several emotional disorders, how to figure out if any of them are a problem for you, and what to do if they are.

Perfectionism is not an emotional disorder. However, just like any other group of people, perfectionists can have emotional disorders. If they do have one, it is in addition to, but separate from, their perfectionism. Most emotional disorders can be treated—but you have to know about them first. If some of the signs (the behaviors, thoughts, and feelings) of perfectionism are similar to the signs of an emotional disorder, then the perfectionism might mask, or hide, the disorder. If it's hidden, it's hard to treat. Think of it this way: If you have allergies, and you get a runny nose, you want to make sure that your runny nose is from the allergies and not from a cold or the flu. That's because you do different things to take care of allergies than you do to take care of a cold or the flu.

The problem isn't just that perfectionism can mask emotional disorders. Perfectionism can also make emotional disorders harder to treat, and emotional disorders can make perfectionism harder to overcome as well.

Only a doctor or therapist can say for sure if you have one of the disorders described in this chapter. If you think you may have any of the problems you read about here, talk to a parent or another trusted adult right away. This person can help find someone who is trained to help you with the problems you are concerned about. You might see a professional like a psychologist, psychiatrist, social worker, or family therapist. It should be a person who will listen to you, and who you feel comfortable talking to. A medical doctor may play a role in your treatment, too.

You can ask friends, relatives, or your doctor if you have one, for advice on finding a professional to see. There is more information about finding a professional in the "Note to Grown-ups." You can read more about getting help and going to therapy in chapter 9.

Sadness, Anger, and Hopelessness

We all have times when we feel sad. That's normal. Usually something has happened: something you tried to do didn't go well, or something bad happened to someone you know. In the same way, there are times when you feel angry. With both these feelings, you eventually feel better. You can go on with life.

Sometimes things pile up and you might start to lose hope. It seems like nothing will work out, or like bad things might happen and you won't be able to stop them. As with sadness and anger, you eventually feel better. Again, this is normal.

If you are a perfectionist, there may be plenty of chances to feel sad, angry, or hopeless. Sometimes nothing seems good enough. You may feel guilty about letting someone down, or frustrated after trying hard and not getting something perfect. You may be angry with someone for making it more difficult for you to do something perfectly.

In these cases, all of the normal feelings you have are made stronger by pressures to be perfect, and by falling short of perfection.

The best thing to do if you are feeling sad, angry, or hopeless is to talk to someone you feel close to. Just connecting with someone in this way will help you feel better. That person may remind you that time goes on, things change for the better, and your feelings are understandable. He or she may also help you find solutions to problems that you are feeling bad about.

Depression

For some people, sad, dark feelings may be even stronger, and they may last for longer periods of time and be harder to overcome.

Thirteen-year-old **Cassie** is having trouble getting up to go to school. After her alarm clock goes off, she lies in bed barely able to think. She has been awake on and off all night, sometimes worrying about things, sometimes hardly being able to think at all. The thought of going to school feels like a giant weight pressing down on her. She has a project due tomorrow for her science class, but she hasn't been able to get herself to work on it for the last few weeks. That doesn't bother her as much as her belief that she wouldn't do very well on it anyway. Cassie has always been an A student, but last fall her grades started to slide big time. Right now, it's time for breakfast, but the thought of eating has no interest for her.

Everyone has ups and downs in their moods, and sometimes the downs can last for several days. If, like Cassie, you've had a down time that has lasted several weeks, you may be depressed. Here are some other possible signs of depression:

- You feel kind of "blah"—nothing interests you and you don't have the energy to do things you usually do.

- You feel sad, or hopeless, or helpless a lot. You might cry a lot.

- Your normal sleep pattern has changed. You sleep a lot, or you sleep very little.

- Your normal eating habits have changed. You eat a lot, or you eat very little.

- You think about death a lot.

- You feel grumpy a lot, or you feel very guilty.

Depression is partly a biological condition, which means your brain works in a certain way because of the chemicals in it. The genes for depression may be passed down from one generation to the next. If you are depressed, there may be other members of your family who also are or have been depressed. The other part of depression is what happens to you. If you have certain experiences growing up (for example, something big that's really sad or scary happens), and you have the genes for depression, you may be depressed.

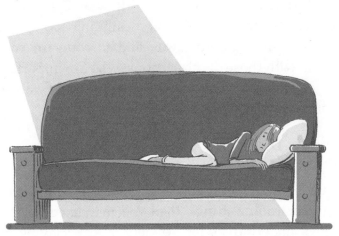

If you or your parents think you might be depressed, it's important to speak to a professional who can find out for sure. Ask your parents or a trusted adult to help you find the right professional. Depression can be treated, and the world can be a lot brighter again. You can read more about treatment on pages 118–124.

Nervousness, Worry, and Fear

Everyone gets nervous at times. Nervousness and worrying are related to fear, and fear is a normal— actually a helpful—human feeling. Fear tells you that something might be wrong, maybe even danger- ous. Fear gets you to pay attention and get ready to defend yourself or get out of the way.

Because of the way perfectionists see themselves, they tend to be nervous, fearful, and worried a lot. "Will I make a perfect grade?" "Will I win the race?" "Will I make a fool of myself?" In chapters 5 and 6 you learned some ways to start thinking about your self-view in a different way and to compare your beliefs with those of other people who are important to you. Doing this can help with the fears and worries that come with perfectionism.

Anxiety Disorder

If you are fearful or nervous most of the time, or if you worry a lot, or especially if your fears often keep you from doing things, then you may have what is called anxiety disorder. Anxiety is fear. Having an anxiety disorder means having fear that seems to control your life. The fear is very strong, you feel it most of the time, and it holds you back so you can't do things you need or want to do.

Carlos has been called the nine-year-old "worrywart," but he doesn't find people's teasing very funny. He can't seem to help himself. For the last couple of years, he has spent a good part of each day worrying about things that might happen. If his dad goes out, will he come back? Will something awful happen to him? When Carlos hands in his homework at school, will the teacher like it? Will she think it's terrible, and will she think Carlos is an idiot? If he goes out to play basketball, will he get hurt? Will he do something stupid and make his team lose?

Because of all this worry, Carlos is typically antsy and grumpy, and he ends up exhausted a lot. He has trouble concentrating on whatever work he is doing, because there is always something to worry about.

Carlos probably has anxiety disorder. This means that his constant worrying, day after day, is something he can't control or talk himself out of. Like depression, anxiety disorder is at least partly bio-logical: Your brain works a certain way because of the chemicals in it. It may be in your family's genes, and if you have certain experiences growing up, this may mean you will have an anxiety disorder.

Perfectionism involves fears that things won't work out well—or that you won't be good enough—but anxiety disorder involves fears about a lot of things. Perfectionists may believe they can make certain things better by being perfect. On the other hand, people with anxiety disorder may feel that most things are beyond their control, and that they *can't* make things better.

Doing Things the "Right" Way

Most people want things done right. They try hard to do work they can be proud of, and they may be disappointed when it doesn't turn out well (or "right"). Some people worry more than others about doing things right, but this worry doesn't usually cause a huge amount of stress.

For perfectionists, doing things right is even more important. If you're a perfectionist, you believe there is absolutely one right way to do things, and you believe you have to do them exactly right in order to feel acceptable. If you do something wrong it shows that you are stupid or something is wrong with you. Doing things the right way is an attempt to control your anxiety and fears about being acceptable. Reading this book will help you find better ways to use some of the energy and time you spend on getting things just right.

Obsessive-Compulsive Disorder

For some people, though, the need for order goes much deeper. It may go so deep that it seems to take over their life.

Elijah, who is eleven, has what seems like an unbreakable habit. When he closes his bedroom door at night, he worries it didn't close completely, so he gets out of bed to check it. After that, he worries more about it, so he has to get up and check it again. He does this again and again, until finally he's so tired he collapses in bed. When Elijah was younger, he felt he had to step only between the cracks in the sidewalk. If he stepped on a crack, he had to go all the way back to where he got on the sidewalk and begin again.

These worries apply to schoolwork as well. Before Elijah starts an assignment, everything on his desk has to be just right—papers straightened, books stacked and straight, three pencils in a row near the back of the desk, one pink eraser sitting up on its edge at the corner. And he has to begin at the beginning and go straight through the assignment to the end, always doing things in a certain order.

Elijah may have what is called Obsessive-Compulsive Disorder, or OCD. The "obsessive" part of this name refers to thoughts and ideas that seem to come into your mind and stay there. You might think about something over and over again. This is called "obsessing" about something. It can be scary and upsetting, and the thoughts don't necessarily seem to be about anything real going on in your life. You might try to get rid of them, but the thoughts keep coming.

The "compulsive" part refers to things you do that you believe have to be done over and over again. Sometimes these repeated actions are meant to fix something you are obsessing about. If you're obsessing about whether the teacher will hate your paper, you might be compulsive about reading the instructions again and again and again—just to be absolutely sure you understand. It may seem like you have to do these things to keep something bad from happening, or just to keep certain thoughts away.

Compulsive behaviors sometimes become little rituals—series of actions that are repeated. Rituals that some kids with OCD have are:

- checking repeatedly to make sure doors are locked

- arranging things in their room a certain way and then repeatedly checking to make sure they did it

- washing their hands over and over

Many perfectionists can be obsessive or compulsive at times or in certain ways. They may set up rituals for themselves that must be followed to keep bad things—possibly failures—from happening. You already know that perfectionists worry a lot about what people will think of them, or about how well they are doing. But when these worries start to take over your life so that the thoughts don't stop and you can't imagine not doing the compulsive behaviors, then OCD may be a problem for you. Perfectionism and OCD can overlap, but they are two different things. Perfectionists try to be perfect to prove that they are good enough. People with OCD tend to do rituals as a way to prevent bad things from happening.

Like anxiety disorder, OCD is partly biological, and also like anxiety disorder, there is usually a lot of fear involved. The obsessive thoughts are usually about the things that are scary. The compulsive behaviors are usually ways to prevent the bad things that the obsessive thoughts are about.

Food Problems

Everyone has foods they like more than others, and most people have foods they absolutely will not eat—even if they have never tried them. So there.

Some people are pickier than other people, but for most people, being picky about food is not a problem. It's only a problem if you don't eat things you need to remain healthy.

Some people's perfectionism shows up in the way they eat food. Some perfectionists decide they can eat only certain foods, or they decide foods have to be eaten in a certain way. They might do this because they believe there is a "correct" diet they should stick with. Even if the food they select is very healthy, the need to be correct can be a real burden. If this is true for you, you can try to overcome it using the exercises in chapter 5.

Eating Disorders

A person's food habits can become a serious problem when they go beyond being picky about food or skipping a meal or two. Sometimes people develop eating disorders—unhealthy habits with food that can lead to serious health problems. Here are some common eating disorders:

- **Anorexia** is when people intentionally eat so little that their bodies don't get enough nutrition.

- **Bulimia** is when people eat normally, or even more than normal, and then make themselves throw up the food. The throwing up is usually kept secret.

- **Binge eating** is when people eat regularly, or maybe lightly, and then eat a large amount of one or more things at a time, in what is called a "binge." Binge eating sometimes goes with bulimia.

- **Emotional eating** is when people overeat in order to feel better emotionally.

Like many of the other disorders described in this chapter, eating disorders involve the chemicals and nerves in the brain, and these may be related to your family's genes. Because of these genes, certain experiences you have may lead to an eating disorder. People with eating disorders often also have depression or anxiety disorder.

Some people with eating disorders are also perfectionists. Such people may believe there are right and wrong ways to eat, or they may be aiming for a certain body shape. For example, they may eat very little so they can lose enough weight to become their idea of the "ideal," or perfect, weight.

The Way You Look

Almost everyone wants to look good. We are surrounded with advertising every day for clothing, jewelry, hair care, makeup, and exercise—all to help us look better. When people are young, they may feel an even stronger need to be attractive. Young people, like everyone, want to be important to others and to be wanted.

Because our society places such a great emphasis on looking a certain way, and especially on being thin, some people start to believe they should be aiming for the "perfect body." It may seem to them like people with less-than-perfect bodies are less acceptable. Some perfectionists may think of their body as something they can try to make perfect, so they can be more acceptable.

Body Dysmorphic Disorder

Some people can't seem to stop worrying about the way they look, and they feel haunted by the idea that something is terribly wrong with their body.

These people may be experiencing Body Dysmorphic (dis-MORE-fik) Disorder (BDD). This is a complicated term that means you can't stop worrying about the shape of your body. Sometimes BDD and eating disorders overlap, such as when people control their eating in order to make some part of their body look a certain way. Many times, though, people with BDD focus on some other part of their body that isn't affected by eating, such as their nose, their hair, or their teeth.

A person with BDD also can experience depression, anxiety disorder, or OCD, and of course he or she can also be a perfectionist. Again, though, perfectionism and BDD are separate things. For perfectionists, the goal is to be liked or accepted—and they may believe that a change in their body is a way to achieve that. People with BDD just think some particular body part doesn't look right. They may not always be looking for personal acceptance, though.

■ ■ ■

Only a doctor or therapist can say for sure if you have one of the disorders described in this chapter. If you think you might have one of these disorders, it's important to talk to an adult so you can get some expert help.

Chapter 9

How Experts Can Help

From reading Part 1 of this book, you know that getting help from grown-ups you trust is an important part of dealing with your never-good-enough feelings. If you think you may have one of the emotional disorders described in chapter 8, or if you feel overwhelmed by your perfectionism, you may need to get some other help, too. You may need to go to counseling or therapy. A counselor or therapist is a person you can talk to about your problems. Here are some common questions people ask about counseling, as well as answers that may help.

#1: What happens in counseling?

Often, the first step in your counseling is to take some tests, called an assessment. The counselor may ask a lot of questions, or he or she may ask you to take a test that involves filling in blanks or saying whether you think something is true or false. You can't pass or fail these tests! They help people figure out what you are like, not how well or poorly you can do. It's important to pay attention to the test and answer the questions truthfully so the person trying to help can get important information. Just try to relax and answer the questions in whatever way you feel is best.

Next, the counselor will want to learn what has been going on for you. He or she might begin by asking why you wanted or needed professional help. Then he or she might ask questions like:

- What kinds of things have you been thinking about?

- How have you been feeling?

- Would you like things to be different?

- If the problems you are concerned about disappeared today, how would your life be different?

You might feel more comfortable in counseling if you know something about the person you are seeing, so feel free to ask your own questions, too. You might ask: Why do I feel this way? How can I change things so I feel better? Will it take a long time?

The counselor will listen to your problems and give you ideas on how to handle them. He or she will ask you questions to learn about your feelings, and together, you can come up with ideas that will help you.

#2: Who will be there?

Your parents or another family grown-up may be with you, or they may not, depending on what you have decided is best. You can decide what makes you feel the most comfortable.

#3: Who will know about this?

It's important for you to know that whatever you say to the counselor, no one—not even your parents—will know what you have talked about unless you say they can. It's all private, so you can say anything you like that you think might help. Ask the counselor how he or she handles your privacy.

The counselor isn't allowed to tell anyone else about your problems, and that includes teachers and other family members. The only time a counselor has to tell your parents about what you say is if you tell the counselor that you're thinking about hurting yourself or someone else, or if someone is hurting you. This is to make sure no one gets hurt, including you. It's up to you whether you tell your friends or anyone else what's going on.

#4: What can my mom or dad do?

The adults who take care of you are concerned about you and want to learn more about how to help you. The counselor can help them understand what's going on with you, how you are doing, and what they can do to help. Counseling often works best if family adults are involved, too.

#5: How long do I have to go to counseling?

Usually when people see a counselor, they go for a session once a week. Depending on what the problems are and what comes up in the course of counseling, you might meet with the counselor for only a few weeks, a few months, or longer. You can always ask your counselor how much longer it might last.

Be patient, because it can take time for counseling to work. It can be very helpful, so stick with it and give it a chance. If it seems like counseling isn't working, talk to your parents and counselor about it.

#6: What about medicine?

In some cases, your counselor might suggest taking medication. Certain medications have been very helpful for people with the emotional disorders discussed in chapter 8. Your counselor will only suggest medication if he or she believes it will help you with an emotional disorder. There are no medications for perfectionism!

Taking medication may seem scary, but it can be helpful. Talk it over with your parents and the counselor. You might talk to your regular doctor, too. If you decide to try medication, remember to follow your counselor's or doctor's instructions, and give it some time. Some people don't notice a difference for a few weeks. For others, it's much quicker. If the medication makes you feel bad, tell someone right away. You might have to go back to the doctor and change how much you take, or try a different medication, or even try more than one medication at the same time. Taking medication can be complicated, because everyone reacts to it a little differently, but if you keep going you'll find something that works for you.

#7: Can I go to counseling for perfectionism?

Counseling is not only for the kinds of emotional disorders described in chapter 8. Many times, people will go to counseling because things just aren't going right in some way, and they would like some help to make life more enjoyable. If something like perfectionism is in your way—if it is making life a burden, or making it hard to get along with others, or if your parents are concerned about you—then meeting with someone who understands these things can be a big help. A counselor can help you get a conversation started with others who are important to you and help you begin to consider different ways of seeing things.

#8: What if we can't afford counseling?

It is possible to find free and low-cost counseling services, depending on your family's needs. You can talk to your school counselor or your principal about special services that you may be able to get through your school district. Your dad or mom can look in the Yellow Pages for low-cost counseling services, or contact a county social worker for more information. Depending on what type of medical insurance your family has, it's possible that the insurance company will help pay the cost of some counseling sessions.

#9: What more can I do?

At the end of this book, you'll find a "Note to Grown-ups" that you can share with your parent or another family adult who can help you with the process of managing your perfectionism. On pages 133–134, you'll find a list of other resources that may be of help to you and your family, too.

■ ■ ■

Counseling is hard work, but it can be worth it. If you have a difficult time with your counseling, tell your counselor and see if you can change what you're doing. Try to remember that counseling isn't something done *to* you—it's something you do *together* with your counselor, and possibly with your parent or parents, too. Lots of people have been in counseling and think it has been extremely helpful. Stay with it, because there is always hope!

Resources

Angelina at the Palace by Katharine Holabird and Helen Craig (New York: Viking, 2005). This is a storybook for younger kids that can be helpful for older kids, too. It gives readers who are interested in learning more about perfectionism a lot to think about.

Don't Feed the Monster on Tuesdays by Adolph Moser (Kansas City, MO: Landmark Editions, 1991). Read about how to raise your self-esteem and have a positive attitude.

The Feelings Book: The Care and Keeping of Your Emotions by Lynda Madison (Middleton, Wisconsin: Pleasant Company, 2002). This book, part of the American Girl Library, explains emotions and provides suggestions for handling powerful feelings and developing positive self-esteem.

KidsHealth
www.kidshealth.org/kid
This Web site for kids can help you learn more about dealing with feelings and staying healthy. Learn more about worries, stress, self-esteem, getting along with parents, and other stuff that can help you with your never-good-enough feelings.

Stick Up for Yourself! Every Kid's Guide to Personal Power and Positive Self-Esteem by Gershen Kaufman, Ph.D., Lev Raphael, Ph.D., and Pamela Espeland (Minneapolis: Free Spirit Publishing, 1999). Simple words and real-life examples show how you can be assertive, be responsible, get along well with others—including your parents—and build your self-esteem.

A NOTE TO GROWN-UPS

It can be very frustrating to watch your child struggling with perfectionism. Whether she is thrashing around with seemingly endless revisions of something, crumbling up in misery over the smallest mistake, or running out of time to do something she is capable of because of a microscopic attention to every detail of the task, it's clear your child is suffering—but nothing you say or do seems to help.

You *can* help. In fact, your child *needs* help from you—she needs you to understand her perfectionism, and to enter into a teamwork process to overcome it. Reading this book together is a start. In this section, you'll get some practical information on what else you can do.

How Do They Get This Way?

Contrary to what might seem logical, perfectionism is not simply a strong need to do well. It's not just being proud of doing well. Perfectionism comes from a deep fear of *not doing well enough*.

Perfectionists worry about this because they have a conviction that being perfect is the only way to be acceptable as a person. For this reason, perfectionism is described as a "relational issue," rather than as something that arises from inside the child. That means it comes about because the child is hoping to prove himself or herself to someone. Because parents have the most emotionally intimate, continuous relationships that their children experience early on, parents always have a large role in their children's emotional development. Kids make sense out of their world—they come to conclusions about who they are and what others expect of them—by adapting to what they find at home.

As a parent—or as another important adult in the child's life—you want your child to do well and be successful in life. Doing things to help make that happen is a part of responsible parenting. Often, though, your hopes for your child's success are interpreted by the child as expectations. This is where it gets complicated: children learn what is expected of them, but they may have questions about what will happen if they don't live up to the expectations. Some kids conclude that they won't be as acceptable to their parents, and this could be where the struggle for perfection begins.

Parents don't always realize how a child interprets their expectations. Becoming aware of this is a vital first step to helping your child overcome perfectionism.

How You Can Help

It can be disheartening at first to realize that you and others in the family play a role in your child's perfectionism, but it's actually good news. It means you can play a role in overcoming it. You *do* have powerful emotional influence in your child's life, and if you can help him feel understood and hopeful, you can help him change.

And that is the essential point: helping your child to overcome perfectionism is not about finding the right thing to do, it's about creating an environment of acceptance. If kids can feel acceptable—loved, cherished, and appreciated—regardless of how well they do something, then not only will perfectionism fade, but their ability to improve will be enhanced as well.

Building an environment of acceptance is a process with several facets. Following are some important things you can do.

See Things the Way Your Child Does

Try to understand the world through your child's eyes. It may seem silly to you, for example, that she is so overly concerned about the two points she lost on a test in school, but if she sees the missed points as an imperfection that threatens her sense of acceptance as a person, then her anxiety makes more sense. The problem is not that she is "wrong," and if you explain to her that it's silly she will only feel worse. The problem is her underlying belief about what it takes to be acceptable. Ask her to talk with you about what her viewpoint is. Accept that for what it is, and then do what you can to reassure her that you do love her and respect her—and that you feel that way for reasons that have nothing to do with the grades she gets.

Engage in Self-Reflection

In spite of the best intentions, parents can send unwanted messages to their children regarding their expectations. It's important for you to examine what messages you are sending. This kind of self-reflection can be hard to do, and in most cases it helps to do it with your partner or spouse. It is not a way of pointing a finger of blame at yourself or your partner. The idea is not to look for a culprit, but to look for the ways you may have influenced your child's self-view. If your child has a negative self-view, you have the power to change things for the better.

Here are some questions you can ask yourself:

- Am I frequently critical of things or people?

- Do I look for and comment on things that aren't quite right?

- Do I "hover" over my children to see that everything is done correctly?

- Do I ever comment on what I appreciate?

It's also helpful to think about your own history: what did your parents expect from you, and how did they convey the message? Another thing to consider is whether there has been any arguing, fighting, violence, or other emotionally upsetting incidents in the home. Children are very sensitive to interpersonal relations in the home and they react, although sometimes only inwardly, to tensions and problems. If there is emotional turmoil in the home, it can't help but affect children, some of whom will strive for perfection in the hopes that it will divert attention onto all the good things perfection seems to promise.

Many of these issues are for you and your spouse or partner to think about and talk over in private. In many cases, they are also enormously helpful parts of a healing dialogue you can have with your child.

Have a Dialogue with Your Child

When you have a true dialogue, where you and your child are talking *and* listening to one another, you do two things: you make it more likely that problems can get solved, and, by paying attention to each other, you show that you are important to each other. Feeling important to you—that is, feeling acceptable to you as a person—is crucial to your child.

In this book, I have suggested to your child that he or she find ways to start such a dialogue. The exercises kids do here will provide ample subject matter for conversation. You could ask about those exercises, or you could suggest other topics. I've also recommended routine family meetings (and in some cases private meetings between you and the child who is reading this book), so that everyone can rely on a forum to explore ideas.

These dialogues might be difficult, but they are worth the effort. Your child may bring up some emotional issues, such as anger or sadness about how things have gone in the past. It's important for you to simply hear what your child says, without making excuses or downplaying it. If you become aware that you have played a role in painful interactions, an apology can help your child in powerful ways. For example, you might say, "Now that I think of it, you're right, I am usually criticizing one thing or another, and I guess I haven't told you why I'm proud of you! I'm really sorry for that." When you apologize, you set the stage for positive change. You have given your child a true gift. If you can say, "I'm sorry for this mistake; I'll work on that and make a difference," then your child can also begin to see that mistakes can be looked at and learned from, and they are not signs of flawed character. This kind of dialogue then becomes an anti-perfectionism vaccine.

This is not easy, of course. No one is totally comfortable owning up to mistakes, and in fact this discomfort is one of the sources of perfectionism. You may feel some shame and embarrassment. This can be a part of the dialogue: "I'm sad and embarrassed about this, and it's hard to talk about, but you're important to me so I'll talk about it with you even though it's hard." It's okay if you struggle with this a bit or don't say everything you want smoothly. The conversation is vital, but it doesn't have to be perfect.

Encourage Your Child

In our current culture, we're good at pointing out errors and things that are done wrong, but we are not always so good at pointing out things that are done well. It is important for your children to have a clear idea that they are valued, not for what they can do (although you are understandably proud of that), but for the simple fact that they are here. Telling your kids what you appreciate about them, thanking them for things they have done, participating with them in their sense of pride or disappointment about something are all ways of letting them know they are cherished and hold an important place in your life. They are ways of affirming and validating your children and helping them feel acceptable. It is called the encouragement process, and there is no such thing as too much of it.

It is only when people feel acceptable as people that a mistake can be just a mistake. If they don't feel acceptable, or if they have questions about that, a mistake seems more like a reflection of some inherent flaw. The resulting anxiety will always make things worse, not better.

For more information on all of these aspects of creating an environment of acceptance, and on perfectionism in general, you can consult my book for parents, *Freeing Our Families from Perfectionism* (see page 133).

Mental Health Issues

I've explained in this book that sometimes the behaviors, thoughts, and feelings that characterize perfectionism can, in their more intense forms, also signify emotional or mental health issues. Perfectionism is simply a personality constellation, or group of particular personality traits, not a form of mental illness. It can, however, be accompanied by emotional disorders. Conditions such as depression, anxiety disorder, or Obsessive-Compulsive Disorder can look a lot like perfectionism, and they can also make perfectionism harder to overcome. Likewise, perfectionism can make these conditions harder to overcome. All of these conditions can be treated with counseling, medication, or a combination of the two, and they should be treated if they exist. Overcoming perfectionism will become easier if these other conditions are addressed in the meantime.

Getting Professional Help

If you have attempted to address your child's perfection-ism, especially with the approach suggested here, and your child remains stuck, feels overwhelmingly hopeless, or can't seem to give up rituals of repetition or extreme orderliness, a psychological assessment may be in order.

A psychological assessment is the first step in get-ting professional help. They are best done by trained and licensed professionals; psychologists have the most extensive training in mental health assessments. If the assessment indicates that a mental disorder is present, there are several options for treatment. In many cases, the person who does the assessment can also do therapy or recommend someone who can. Psychologists, psy-chiatrists, social workers, marriage and family therapists, counselors, nurse-practitioners, and pastoral counselors may be trained to do psychotherapy and family therapy. If medications are needed for conditions like depression or anxiety disorders, or if hospitalization is necessary for conditions like advanced eating disorders, the services of a medically trained psychiatrist will be required. Licenses, degrees, and levels of training can vary greatly.

The best way to find a professional to help you or your child is to ask trusted friends or family members if they know of someone they'd recommend. If no friend or family member can give you suggestions, here are some other ways you can find one:

- Ask your doctor or other health care professionals for references.

- Ask your child's teacher or school counselor, who can draw on experience from their consultations with mental health professionals about students.

- Ask a member of the clergy from your religious faith.

- Ask people in any support group you might belong to, such as a parenting group, Alcoholics Anonymous, or Al-Anon.

If no one you know personally can give you leads, you can also call one of the professional associations listed on pages 133–134. They often have lists of professionals in local areas. Let them know if cost is a concern; ask if free or low-cost services are available.

Make sure you and your child feel listened to and respected by the person you consult; if you don't, try someone else.

Before treatment begins, find out how you will be part of the process. Except for the details of any particular session, which are covered by privacy rules, you should be informed about your child's progress. This may be done in a separate session with you, or you may be included in one or more of your child's sessions.

A Word of Encouragement

Thank you for sharing this book with your child, and for having the courage to examine what the issue of perfectionism has meant to you. As your child's parent, or as an adult who is close to the child in question, you have the power to change things for the better. Working together with your child on this will strengthen the bonds between you, and it will lay the groundwork for freeing your child, and perhaps yourself, from perfectionism. Best wishes on the journey!

Other Resources and References

Adderholdt, Miriam, and Jan Goldberg. *Perfectionism: What's Bad About Being Too Good?* (Minneapolis: Free Spirit Publishing, 1999).

Amen, Daniel G., and Lisa C. Routh. *Healing Anxiety and Depression* (New York: G.P. Putnams' Sons, 2003).

Antony, Martin M., and Richard P. Swinson. *When Perfect Isn't Good Enough* (Oakland, CA: New Harbinger Publications, Inc., 1998).

Dewyze, Jeannette, and Allan Mallinger. *Too Perfect: When Being In Control Gets Out of Control* (New York: Ballantine Books, 1992).

Dinkmeyer, Don, and Gary D. McKay. *Raising a Responsible Child* (New York: Fireside, 1996).

Greenspon, Thomas S. *Freeing Our Families from Perfectionism* (Minneapolis: Free Spirit Publishing, 2002).

Organizations

American Academy of Child and Adolescent Psychiatry
(202) 966-7300
www.aacap.org

American Psychiatric Association HealthyMinds.org
1-888-357-7924
www.healthyminds.org

American Psychological Association Help Center
1-800-374-2721
www.apahelpcenter.org

Anna Westin Foundation
(952) 361-3051
www.annawestinfoundation.org
For the prevention and treatment of eating disorders.

Canadian Psychiatric Association
(613) 234-2815
www.cpa-apc.org

Canadian Psychological Association
1-888-472-0657
www.cpa.ca

National Alliance on Mental Illness
1-800-950-6264
www.nami.org

National Association of Social Workers
1-800-638-8799
www.naswdc.org

National Institute of Mental Health
1-866-319-4357
www.nimh.nih.gov

Index

About the Author

Thomas S. Greenspon, Ph.D., is a licensed psychologist and licensed marriage and family therapist in private practice in Minneapolis, Minnesota, where he counsels families, couples, children, adolescents, and adults. He earned a B.A. from Yale and a Ph.D. in psychology from the University of Illinois in 1968.

Tom lectures and writes on a variety of topics, including the emotional needs of gifted children and adults. He is a member of several professional organizations and has authored dozens of articles about perfectionism, the self-experience of gifted individuals, and couples' and family relations.

Tom is married to Barbara C. Greenspon, M.A., his partner in private practice. They are former copresidents of the Minnesota Council for the Gifted and Talented (MCGT) and served on the Minnesota State Advisory Committee for Gifted. Tom is the recipient of the 1998 MCGT Award for Distinguished Service to Gifted Individuals.

Other Great Books from Free Spirit

What to Do When You're Scared & Worried
A Guide for Kids
by James J. Crist, Ph.D.
From a dread of spiders to panic attacks, kids have worries and fears, just like adults. This is a book kids can turn to when they need advice, reassurance, and ideas. For ages 9–13.
$9.95, 128 pp., 2-color illust., Softcover, $5^{3}/_{8}$" x $8^{3}/_{8}$".

What to Do When You're Sad & Lonely
A Guide for Kids
by James J. Crist, Ph.D.
All kids feel sad and lonely sometimes. Growing numbers of children are living with depression, a disease often mistaken for sadness. This reassuring book offers strategies and tips kids can use to beat the blues and blahs, get a handle on their feelings, make and keep friends, and enjoy their time alone. For ages 9–13.
$9.95, 128 pp., 2-color illust., Softcover, $5^{3}/_{8}$" x $8^{3}/_{8}$".

Speak Up and Get Along!
Learn the Mighty Might, Thought Chop, and More Tools to Make Friends, Stop Teasing, and Feel Good About Yourself
by Scott Cooper
A handy toolbox of ways to get along with others, this book presents 21 strategies kids can learn and use to express themselves, build relationships, end arguments and fights, halt bullying, and beat unhappy feelings. For ages 8–12.
$12.95, 128 pp., 2-color illust., Softcover, 6" x 9".

Get Organized Without Losing It
by Janet S. Fox
Kids today have a lot to keep track of—and keep organized. Schoolwork, activities, chores, backpacks, lockers, desks…and what about fun? Here's help for kids who want to manage their tasks, their time, and their stuff without going overboard. For ages 8–13.
$8.95, 112 pp., 2-color illust., Softcover, $5^{1}/_{8}$" x 7".

To place an order or to request a free catalog of Self-Help for Kids® and Self-Help for Teens® materials, please write, call, email, or visit our Web site:

Free Spirit Publishing Inc.
**217 Fifth Avenue North • Suite 200 • Minneapolis, MN 55401
toll-free 800.735.7323 • local 612.338.2068
fax 612.337.5050 • help4kids@freespirit.com • www.freespirit.com**

Fast, Friendly, and Easy to Use
www.freespirit.com

Browse the catalog

Info & extras

Many ways to search

Quick check-out

Stop in and see!

Our Web site makes it easy to find the positive, reliable resources you need to empower teens and kids of all ages.

The Catalog.
Start browsing with just one click.

Beyond the Home Page.
Information and extras such as links and downloads.

The Search Box.
Find anything superfast.

Your Voice.
See testimonials from customers like you.

Request the Catalog.
Browse our catalog on paper, too!

The Nitty-Gritty.
Toll-free numbers, online ordering information, and more.

The 411.
News, reviews, awards, and special events.

 Our Web site is a secure commerce site. All of the personal information you enter at our site—including your name, address, and credit card number—is secure. So you can order with confidence when you order online from Free Spirit!

For a fast and easy way to receive our practical tips, helpful information, and special offers, send your email address to upbeatnews@freespirit.com. View a sample letter and our privacy policy at www.freespirit.com.

1.800.735.7323 • fax 612.337.5050 • help4kids@freespirit.com